The Great War from the German Trenches

THE GREAT WAR FROM THE GERMAN TRENCHES

A Sapper's Memoir, 1914–1918

Artur H. Boer

Translated and edited by
Bertil van Boer *and*
Margaret L. Fast

McFarland & Company, Inc., Publishers
Jefferson, North Carolina

Frontispiece: Artur Hermann Boer (1893–1967) in 1965 (courtesy van Boer family archives).

LIBRARY OF CONGRESS CATALOGUING-IN-PUBLICATION DATA

Names: Boer, Artur H., author. | Van Boer, Bertil H., translator, editor. | Fast–Van Boer, Margaret L., translator, editor.
Title: The Great War from the German trenches : a sapper's memoir, 1914–1918 / Artur H. Boer ; translated and edited by Bertil van Boer and Margaret L. Fast–van Boer.
Description: Jefferson, North Carolina : McFarland & Company, Inc., Publishers, 2016. | Includes bibliographical references and index.
Identifiers: LCCN 2016026689 | ISBN 9781476663685 (softcover : acid free paper) ∞
Subjects: LCSH: Boer, Artur H. | World War, 1914–1918—Personal narratives, German. | World War, 1914–1918—Campaigns—Western Front. | Soldiers—Germany—Biography. | Germany. Heer—Biography.
Classification: LCC D640 .B5834 2016 | DDC 940.4/1343092 [B]—dc23
LC record available at https://lccn.loc.gov/2016026689

ISBN (print) 978-1-4766-6368-5
ISBN (ebook) 978-1-4766-2392-4

BRITISH LIBRARY CATALOGUING DATA ARE AVAILABLE

© 2016 Bertil H. van Boer and Margaret L. Fast. All rights reserved

No part of this book may be reproduced or transmitted in any form or by any means, electronic or mechanical, including photocopying or recording, or by any information storage and retrieval system, without permission in writing from the publisher.

On the cover: Artur Boer at the front in uniform in 1915 (family archives); German soldiers in a trench between 1914 and 1918 (Library of Congress)

Printed in the United States of America

McFarland & Company, Inc., Publishers
 Box 611, Jefferson, North Carolina 28640
  www.mcfarlandpub.com

To the memory of
Artur's eldest son,
Alf Bertil Herman van Boer
(1924–2014)

Table of Contents

Foreword by Hans Boer   1
Introduction by the Editors   3
Author's Original Preface to the Memoir   53

1. The Call to Arms: A Mother   55
2. 1915: Meeting in No Man's Land   60
3. June 15, 1915: The First Attack   62
4. The Battle for Rózan: July 18–24, 1915   77
5. Transport to the Hospital   84
6. A Time of Convalescence   87
7. Back to the Barracks   92
8. France on the Western Front   94
9. The Stalemate in Champagne   96
10. Aisne in Champagne   100
11. Dirt, Lice, and Clay   102
12. We Do Not Live by Bread Alone   106
13. Verdun—The Battle at the Bois de Caillette on Ascension Day, June 1, 1916   112
14. Comrade Karl Höhle *In Memoriam*   118
15. The Ammunition Distributor in Champagne   120
16. Outside Verdun Once Again   124
17. The Marne Offensive: Breakthrough at the Chemins des Dames   132
18. Attack at the Crozat Canal   137

Table of Contents

19. The Argonne, 1918	143
20. The Red Baron	148
21. The Offensive at the Marne	154
22. French Tank Attack	156
23. The Americans Arrive	169
24. The Last Events and Close	181
Index	187

May all who read my work
be united in a single thought:
My fondest desire that seizes my heart
and moves it to tears is simply:
No war ever again!

Artur H. Boer

Foreword
by Hans Boer

The First World War (1914–1918) lies a century behind us, but like the Second World War should never be forgotten; the events from the beginning of our previous century deserve to be included in our memories. Of course, the methods of waging war were not as consciously grim as in the wars of later times, but nonetheless were the cause of enormous suffering and tragedy. Millions of families were split apart, children lost their fathers and wives their husbands, and a huge number of people were lost. Just like the Second World War, the First World War altered people's picture of the world at large, and as in all wars apparently "meaningless" events were actually important to understanding the realities of war. For the "little man," for you and me, these realities of war are unfathomable and incomprehensible. Chronicles of war that we usually read are often reconstructed, dramatized, and romanticized. Often the horrors are described for the sake of the horror itself and to provide an approximation of the violence and blood. The present book, without excuse or exaggeration, documents the everyday aspects of war. It is the memoir and reflections from the trenches and battlefield of a frontline soldier during a particularly bloody epoch. This book gives us the occasion to place ourselves directly into the action, as seen from a sapper's perspective.

Artur H. Boer (1893–1967), my father and the author of this book, moved after the end of the war from Germany to Sweden, where he lived in Kumla and Karlskoga, among other places. His experiences during the war left deep scars in his soul, and like the majority who have survived war up close, his eyes spoke of his experiences. For him,

Foreword

this book was a means of organizing his memories, and thus with it he has provided a worthwhile addition to the literature of the First World War.

As can be seen in several passages in the book, he was a lover of music, and in both Kumla and Karlskoga he played viola in the local orchestras. Otherwise, he worked in a shoe factory in Kumla and in Karlskoga at Bofors up to his retirement. In 1960, when he was pensioned, he began to write down his memoirs, and they remained unpublished apart from excerpts in the local Karlskoga newspaper, *Nerikes Allehanda,* in 1965. These memoirs are what you hold in your hands.

Let all of us, without reservation, concur with the ardent wish of my father that introduces this book—"No war ever again"—a valid sentiment to this day.

Introduction by the Editors

About the Book
BY BERTIL H. VAN BOER

I knew my grandfather. Such a statement ought to seem rather obvious, but for me it entailed a cross-cultural story that transcended nations and continents. I was born and raised in the United States, some five years or so after my father emigrated from Sweden. As a child, I knew little about my grandfather still back in the Old World (and nothing about my paternal grandmother, which is another story entirely), and it was not until I was twelve years old that we traveled to Europe and I met him for the first time. We were immediately drawn to each other, although we could not communicate in a normal fashion; at that time I spoke virtually no German or Swedish, and he knew only a few fleeting words of English, but my uncle Hans and my aunt Ulla, who spoke English quite well, acted as translators, as did my father. This made no difference to my grandfather, for he doted on my brother and me for the two weeks we spent in the town of Karlskoga where he lived. I played violin with and for him, learned some words and phrases in both his languages, and after we left, corresponded with him for several years until his death in 1967. In his letters, even in his seventies, he learned to write in English, after a fashion, and by that time I was becoming adept at German (the Swedish did not come until long after he died). These letters were about everyday life, and I later learned that he always awaited them with great anticipation.

I did not know until later that he too had been an immigrant. He was born in the Prussian town of Jarotschin (Jarocin in today's Poland) in 1893. His father—my great-grandfather—was an engineer for the

Introduction

Royal Prussian State Railways and his mother—my great-grandmother, born Klara Kluge—came from a prominent Prussian family outside of Posen, then likewise a city in Prussia. I know little of his early life, save that he lost his mother early—how or why still remains a mystery to be solved—but that he was raised to some degree by his stepmother, Lina Springer, who my great-grandfather had married after his divorce from his first wife. In this second family, he also had a half-sister, Martel, who he adored (and who I later also met in Mainz as a child, but she does not come into this story). Artur was well-trained as an engineer in Berlin at the Royal Academy of Engineering, as well as becoming a proficient violinist by taking instruction at the Royal Prussian Academy of Music. He was apparently incredibly gifted as a musician (eventually preferring the viola over the violin), but when he pressed to make it his career, the story goes that his father, a rather staunch and severe man, took his violin and smashed it over his knee, telling him in essence that this was no fit occupation for a productive human being. Or at least, that is the story I heard as a child. When he was recruited into the German army as one of the Pioneer Corps in 1914, he had already settled upon engineering as his occupation, having shortly before received his diploma from the Royal Academy of Engineering. He never lost his deep love for music, however, and even during the war continued to perform.

By the end of the war, having been wounded and gassed, he was disillusioned with both politics and war, and his return home to a distressed Berlin brought the futility of everything connected with World War I into focus. By 1920 he had enough of the depression and inflation that wracked his homeland and immigrated to Sweden. There he re-established his life, where he married my grandmother, Elsa Linnea Orest, in Karlskoga in 1922 and began work as a civil engineer. His life there, however, was not entirely calm, even though he continued to play his violin in the local orchestras and worked successfully for several firms, ironically enough including Bofors, one of the world's leading manufacturers of weapons produced by a nation that has remained neutral in two world wars. Just as history repeats itself, so did his own life story; he divorced my grandmother and sent my father off into the military at the age of 13 (where he too was trained as an engineer/architect and as a musician, this time as a flautist and conductor in the latter field—again, another tale). He remarried, had another family (my aunt, uncle, and a flock of wonderful cousins), and because Sweden was neutral during World War II, in his new home he was able to escape the devastation that occurred in the rest of Europe. This meant a comfortable, if staid, life in central Sweden in a house that he himself designed and built, and later in an apartment as he grew older and had health problems.

While this brief biography does not do him justice—after all, his experiences and path were as kaleidoscopic as anyone might wish—it does place him into perspective. Artur Hermann Boer (or, to give him the name on his birth registration, Hermann Artur Böer) was a man of many facets, and it is his sense of immediate history that is reflected in this memoir of the First World War, now a century past. He experienced and he observed, but not the overall geopolitical struggles or the vast historical perspective that historians have studied. Rather, his view was one from the trenches, a person who was often in the thick of things and saw first-hand what war meant to the average human being, be they friend or foe. Moreover, he found time among the many jobs his company of engineers or sappers had to do to maintain a journal. This was written in a unique brand of shorthand he developed himself, although based upon the well-known Gabelsberger method he learned during his convalescence. One might be surprised that, amid the falling shells, the nitty-gritty struggle of trench warfare, and the constant agony of human suffering he encountered day by day on the front, he had the time not only to scribble down his experiences in cursory form, he also took with him, in addition to his violin, a portable camera to record for posterity snippets of the life described in the journal. Some of these photographs from our family collection have been included in this book, published for the first time. The journal itself became the source of this memoir, and the photos that he kept alongside it may only be a tithe of those he actually took; no doubt a number have disappeared over the years since they were taken. As one reads through this, it may seem that the descriptions are more intimate and focused, and events that took place often over the course of years (as so often happens in trench warfare) are sometimes telescoped and perhaps even lacunar. His style of writing was journalistic, not prosaic, his observations scattered as the varied experiences happened to him, for he never knew what would come next. It is immediate, sometimes mundane, as war often is, and sometimes technical, as befits his position

Introduction

as an engineer within the German army, and, most importantly, it is always human. Curiously enough, even the enemy seems (with one rather glaring exception) to be depicted as human as well, for he was no zealot and had little use for political posturing, either pro- or anti-war.

A century has now passed since World War I, euphemistically called "the war to end all wars," and from the hindsight of the twenty-first century, it seems not much has changed. His admonition—"No war ever again"—remains a potent, yet forlorn cry in the wilderness of geopolitical conflict that robs us of our common humanity, not to mention being proven over and over again that war is inconsequential in the ultimate unfolding of human history. As noted in his journal, the people to people contact always seems to work out just fine when no one has a rigid ideology or political-nationalist agenda to follow. In his own experience, the Germans were often considered to be the "enemy" in the places he served, but they are nonetheless given hospitality by the vanquished in France and seek to trade with soldiers of the opposing armies during lulls in the fighting, as if their combat was merely a job to be done, not a life choice or creed. The people he meets are ordinary human beings, not famous people (although there is a brief encounter with a member of the squadron of the notorious Baron von Richthofen, who he also saw battling in the skies above his trench), and their stories are paramount, for in the listing of battles, the maps of the changing front lines east and west, and the generals and politicians who drove the war, these individuals who risked their lives and often died are silently relegated to mass graves or fields of anonymous white crosses; occasionally, their names would be carved on monuments in their hometowns, but the lives that they could have led, the accomplishments for the benefit of society that could have been made, or the self-determination of their own destiny were all unrealized. This senseless result is the core meaning behind his admonition. In his view, there were no real enemies in a literal sense, rather only men on both sides who served the war machine that wreaked such havoc among the empires of that time, and were continually to do so thereafter in the decades that followed up to and including our own time. It was Artur's hope in turning his journal into a memoir that humanity would accept the lessons of the human scale of the destruction and learn from it, a hope that he maintained until his own death.

About the Book (Bertil H. van Boer)

Finally, one requires a word about this book and its translation. As already noted, a journal was kept by my grandfather diligently throughout the war, and he retained it later on only as a memorial to the sacrifices he made during those four years of his youth. He did not even look at it again for many years afterwards, mainly because it contained memories that were painful, and he sought to suppress his own past as much as possible. As an immigrant in a foreign land, he probably also felt that Swedes, including his own children born in that country, would have little context or use for the material it contained. It was indeed only in the 1960s that he felt comfortable enough to consider turning it into a memoir by first translating his journal into Swedish, creating a more fluid narrative than the cursory shorthand contained, and releasing portions of it in a series of articles in the local Karlskoga newspaper. It was always his intention that the entire work (which he titled "Violence and Crime") was to be published complete as a memoir, which is probably also why he carefully retained some photographs from his years on the front. His work, therefore, must be considered a memoir, but it is based almost exclusively upon a journal that dates from the First World War. This work is thus a dual-layered translation, from his unique shorthand (a sort of code that only he himself knew and could decipher) to German, and from German into Swedish, the last of which he never did speak without a heavy German accent, according to my aunt and uncle (me being too young and not fluent enough at the time I knew him to know differently). It is therefore not surprising that his written Swedish final version, sent to my father in typescript, is imperfect and often unidiomatic, with many terms that cross the boundaries of language. By translating it into English, yet another layer has been added. We have, however, endeavored to retain the brevity of his often rapid-fire writing style while correcting the obvious grammatical and syntactical errors, only here and there connecting what originally were separate sentences or loose phrases so that the flow of the language makes some sense to modern English readers. We have not opted to "update" any of the descriptions, for this would erase what he himself saw, or thought he saw, even though there might be a more historically-accurate analysis or description. Thus, the work is immediately historical, but the historical truth contained therein is from a subjective point of view that reflects the observations, sights, and comments from someone on the ground, regardless of whether the larger truth might have been viewed differently from an *ex post facto* scholarly perspective. We hope that you, the reader, therefore will see his raw and unfiltered observations as on-the-ground realism, giving a portrait that will put meaning into his creed—"No war ever again." It is not Erich Maria Remarque's *All Quiet on the Western Front*, nor is it a gripping novel with plot, characters (although, of course, there are many "characters" within), or effusive and lengthy description of now-exotic locations. Nor is the focus always on the grim, grisly sights that must have been visible to him on a continual basis in the trenches. To provide the historical context and framework, a substantial introduction has been added that presents the information that allows for the setting within the larger historical picture, referring directly to various passages within the memoir itself. It is our hope that this work will not only be of historical value, it will also provide an understanding of one of the great tragedies of the world as witnessed by one who survived it and wrote about it as it was happening.

This memoir has been the result of the collaboration of several people. The memoir itself is, of course, the sole work of Artur H. Boer, and I, as his grandson, have dedicated it to his eldest son, my late father, Alf Bertil H. van Boer. My uncle and Artur's youngest son, Hans Boer, wrote the foreword originally for an unpublished Swedish version of the memoir. Both this and the memoir itself were translated by myself and my wife, Margaret L. Fast, who also wrote most of the Introduction. I would also like to express my appreciation to Esther Gilbert, wife of the late Sir Martin Gilbert, whose maps we have been given permission to include because they focus on exactly those geographical areas along the fronts where my grandfather was stationed. In addition, my thanks goes out to the folks at Taylor & Francis for extending their permission and blessing, as well.

Artur H. Boer and His Times
by Margaret L. Fast

Artur Boer provides his reader with an eminently readable account of his service in the German military during World War I. His memoir is unusual in that he was stationed on both the Eastern and Western fronts. As Vejas Liulevicius states:

During the First World War, the experiences of German soldiers on the Western and Eastern Fronts seemed worlds apart. These separate worlds shaped distinct "Front-Experiences" (even for soldiers who fought on both fronts) which proved to have important consequences both during and after the war, testimony to the impact of war on culture. While all was "quiet on the Western Front," a routine of hell of mud, blood, and shell shock in the trenches, a different ordeal took shape for the millions of German troops in the East from 1914 to 1918. What they saw among largely unfamiliar lands and peoples, both at the front and in the vast occupied areas behind the lines, left durable impressions.[1]

Not long after Germany declared war on Russia on August 1, 1914, Artur Boer became one of the 683,722 (1914–1915) and then 1,316,235 (1915–1916) soldiers who fought on the Eastern Front.[2] He was twenty-two and a newly minted engineer when he begins his memoir. He was recruited into the German Army as a sapper and served in many locations on both fronts, giving his experiences a broad geographical sweep.[3]

Geography

The memoir begins after basic training with the company troop train traveling from his garrison town in spring of 1915, most probably Stettin near Berlin (which he refers to later on). They head initially to Allenstein, and then on to Thorn by way of Danzig (see Figure 1).[4] Allenstein (Olsztyn), now located in northeastern Poland, became part of the German Empire in 1871 and was connected to Thorn in 1873 by railroad. Although Artur did not fight in the famous Battle of Tannenberg, one of the first major engagements of the war on the Eastern Front that took place August 26–30, 1914, he mentions his location in relationship to it: "Now we weren't so very far from the border in East Prussia where not so long ago Hindenburg drowned thousands of Russians. Think, what a great battle!"

On June 15, 1915, they are to take and hold a position north of Prasznic on the so-called Czerwena Gora (Black Road). His company held positions in this area, and the German army took the village of Szla, some 60 miles north of Warsaw. The Russians began to use a scorched earth policy and burned everything as they evacuated. When the Russians torched the villages of Podossje and Plonjava on the Orzic River, the engineers were instructed to build a new wooden bridge to replace the one destroyed. After crossing the river they encountered daily skirmishes along the way to the city of Rózan.

Introduction

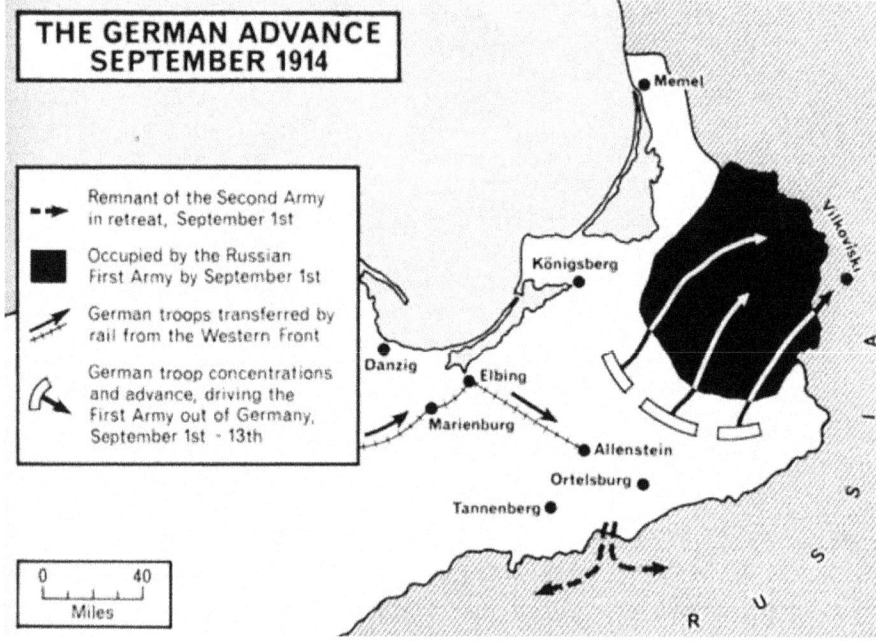

Figure 1. **Map of the German advance on the Eastern Front in September 1914 as described in Artur Boer's memoir (from *The Routledge Atlas of the First World War* [Figure 29] copyright 2002 Sir Martin Gilbert and Routledge, reproduced by permission of Taylor and Francis Books UK and the estate of Sir Gilbert Martin. www.martingilbert.com).**

As they tried to protect themselves from sharpshooters in the forests, they made little progress. On July 17 the German army moved to take Kreuzberg, one of the Imperial Russian fortresses in that town, and after a fierce battle they did. The battle for Rózan on the Narev River takes place July 18–24 and it is at an estate near this city that Artur is first wounded by shrapnel from a cluster bomb. On July 24 he is transported away from the front, first walking back to the town of Prasznic, from which he takes a horse-drawn narrow-gauge train to the German border, and then a train to Osterode and on to Wenigerode in the Harz Mountains to recuperate for eight weeks. Artur then returns to Stettin, his training barracks, and in autumn is assigned to active duty on the Western Front. During this time he was assigned to build pontoon bridges on the Oder River.

Before returning to the war, he takes a home leave to see his family in Berlin, returning shortly thereafter to attend the funeral for his father, who died in October of 1915. This time he travels to the Western Front, passing the French border at the city of Charleville in Champagne to arrive at company headquarters near Tahure (now known as Sommepy-Tahure) near the city of Reims, where the war was stalemated, in late November. Here he joined troops at the Siegfried Front or Line, a portion of the immense system of defenses in northeastern France that extended from Lens to Verdun. It is also here that he spends his first Christmas on the Western Front. After a brief leave in March 1916 he returns to a much more active front in an engagement that occurs in May 1916 near the Aisne River, which was followed by an advance to the Marne in May and June, where the German army broke though at the Chemin des Dames, a road between Laon and Reims. They stayed between the forts of Vaux and Doumont, two defensive positions outside Verdun, and fought a three-hour battle near the Bois de Caillette. This was part of the larger Battle of Verdun (see Figure 2), which took place from February 21 to December 15, 1916, as well as the Battle of the Somme, fought from July 1 to November 18, 1916, near the city of Bapaume, where Artur was stationed.

From January to April of 1917 he was back in Verdun, and at the beginning of 1918 he was moved to an unknown position further along the front, possibly in the same region. March saw his company at work building pontoon bridges on the Somme River between St. Christ and Tergnier, the so-called "Canal de Crozat," also known as the "Canal de Picardie," which formed part of the Hindenburg Line (also known as the Siegfried Line) of German defenses thereafter. He then moves on to the Argonne between the Meuse and Aisne, a place of military stalemate, and then on to encounter the English army between Noyon and Mont Didier along the Siegfried Front (which ranged from Cambrai to the Bapaume) during the Spring Offensive in March 1918 (see Figure 3). He also returned to the Chemin des Dames. This is the second battle of Chemin de Dames, at first a success for the Germans but in the end it was a disaster. In the late summer he was sent to the Meuse River in the Argonne to participate in an active engagement. The last battle on the Meuse took place from September 27 to October 18. It was here that he encountered the recent newcomers to the Allies, the Americans, who joined in the successful attack on the Hindenburg Line. On October 4 the German army had requested an armistice, and retreating

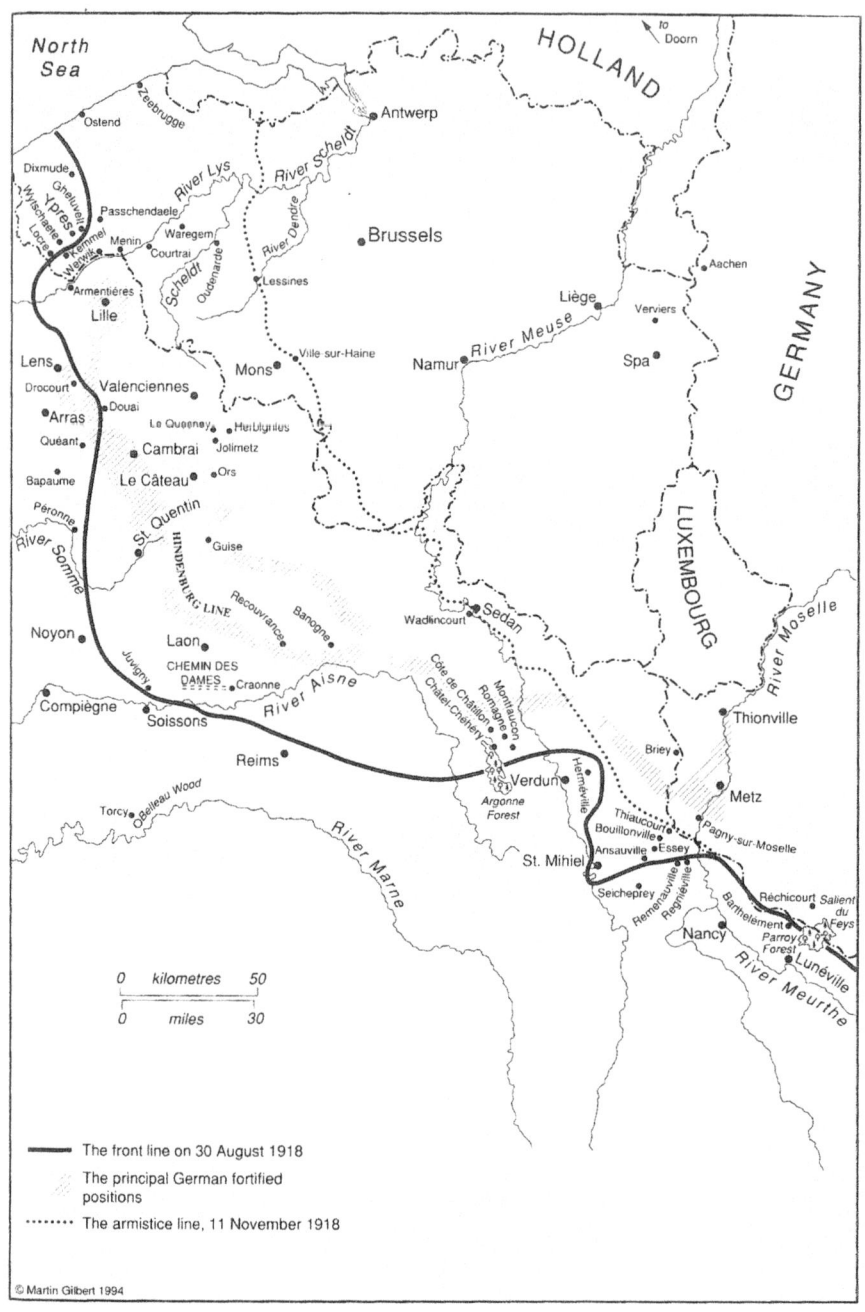

Figure 2. The Western Front, 1915–1916 (from *The First World War* [Figure 21] copyright 1994 Sir Martin Gilbert and Henry Holt, reproduced by permission of Taylor and Francis Books UK and the estate of Sir Gilbert Martin. www.martingilbert.com).

Figure 3. The Western Front, 1918 (from *The First World War* [Figure 25] copyright 1994 Sir Martin Gilbert and Henry Holt, reproduced by permission of Taylor and Francis Books UK and the estate of Sir Gilbert Martin. www.martingilbert.com).

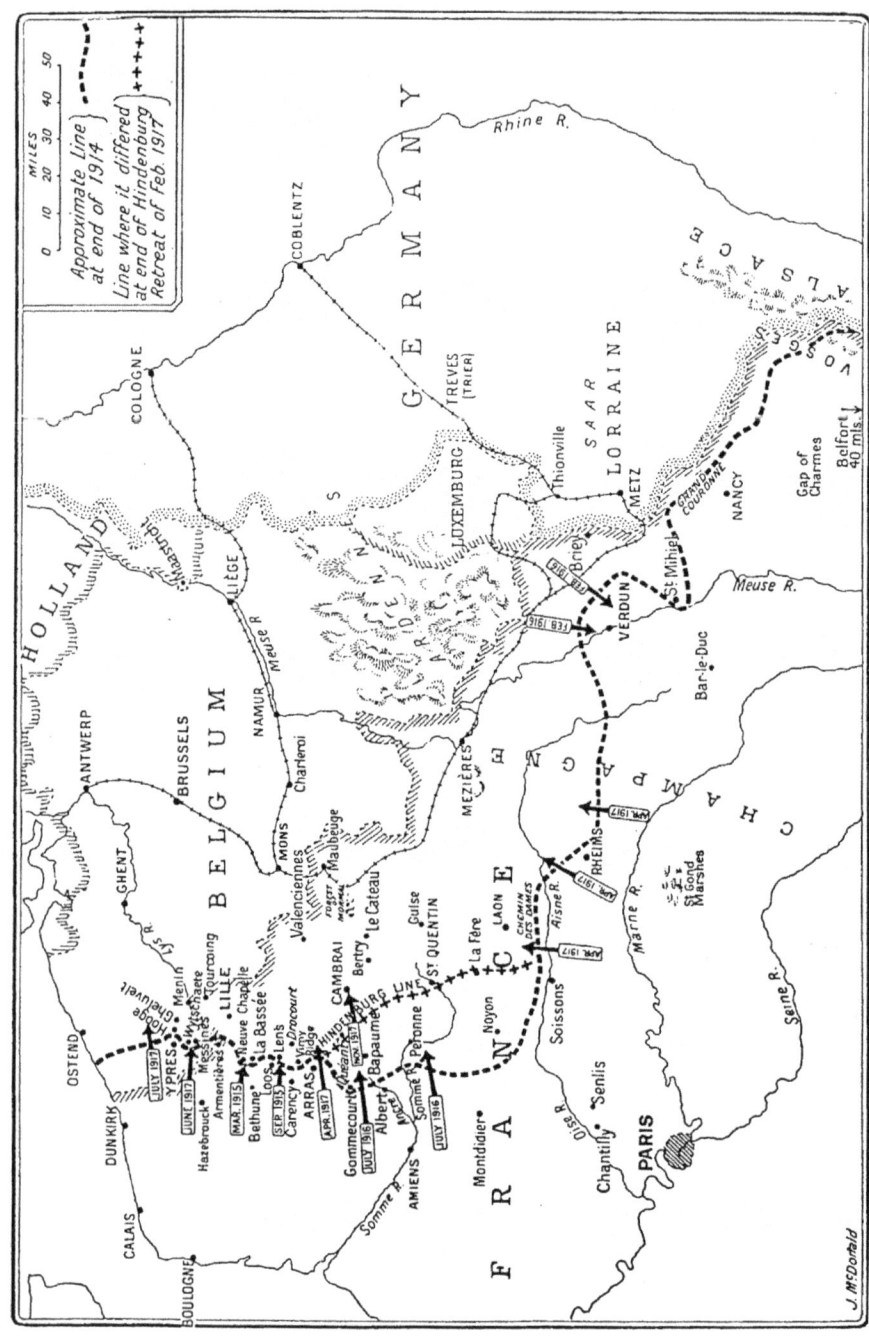

Figure 4. The Western Front from the end of 1914 to the Hindenburg Retreat (map by J. McDonald, reprinted from Basil Liddell Hart, *Reputations* [London: John Murray, 1928]).

troops were marched to the nearest train station in late October. There they were taken in boxcars for a respite in Neunkirchen in the Rhineland, intending to be reassigned to engage the Americans on the Strasbourg front, apparently unaware of the diplomatic overtures that were ongoing to end the war. On November 18, however, while in route they received word that the Kaiser had abdicated and that they were to be diverted back to their home barracks as part of the Armistice agreement reached on November 11. At this point, Artur's memoirs conclude with him returning home to his family in Berlin, apparently being demobilized either in Stettin or along the way.

Though much of the description of the geography is localized within specific trenches or places, Artur does occasionally give some indications of longer distances, generally in kilometers. In the first chapter and occasionally elsewhere, however, he notes a march that takes place in *Meilen,* or miles. These refer to German miles, an old-style measurement each one of which is roughly ten kilometers; thus a three-"mile" march was about 30 kilometers or about 20 American miles long.

The Diverse Enemy

The memoir takes place during a large-scale European war, in which the German army fought various peoples and nations, although much of the action itself was restricted to Western Russia and Northeastern France along more or less static front lines. Initial German advances swept through Belgium and Luxembourg in the west, and Poland in the east, so that areas behind the lines under occupation were relatively quiet (see Figure 4). These various enemies of Germany that Artur encountered were, initially, Russians, and on the Western Front first and foremost the French, as well as their allies, the British and colonial subjects, and eventually the Americans (after 1917).

His interactions with these opponents were not always in combat. For instance, Artur describes a brief armistice one spring morning whereby the German and the Russian soldiers have a "Sunday Promenade" after laying down their grenades. As goods are exchanged, a discussion about politics ensues, in which the combatants arrive at an impasse: "The Russians wanted us to shoot our Kaiser, and we wanted

Introduction

them to hang the Czar." This parallel view of the leaders of the war is followed by a comparison of their rations and reassurance of returning safely with no surprise attack. Artur notes that this is "proof that the people are not the ones who decide on war or peace." Then reality sets in that supersedes the amity between the common soldiers: "Some officer or another got wind of the thing and reported our meeting to his superiors. An hour later officers armed with carbines arrived and posted themselves beside the bunkers with instructions to shoot anyone who dared to leave the trenches for another meeting with the Russians." What had been a momentary truce on a person-to-person level is now thwarted by a higher command. Artur then notes that these soldiers were soon relieved of their positions.

On the Western Front, the main enemy of the Germans is the French, for whom Artur more than once indicates respect. Indeed, in occupied territory, the local people are more than kind to the occupiers, especially those on leave. In one of the last chapters of his memoirs, Artur is grateful for the hospitality the French civilian population:

> We were to pass eight wonderful days of rest far behind the front in a small French village among the civilian population. This was a completely new environment for us, who had for the most time remained in the Champagne or Argonne region. Already, there nature was abundant in this very mountainous region. The village where we stayed was small with narrow streets and squeezed in among the heights. There were natural springs everywhere on the streets and at each watering place the population had placed stone basins where they fetched their water and did their laundry. It was a wonderful, clear water that ran day and night. It fit the nice stone houses and the clean cobblestone streets. It was a real pleasure for us each morning to be able to bathe in the ice-cold, clear water. The population itself where we were quartered showed an open sympathy for us from the first moment. Despite the poverty that these people live in—the majority of the villagers worked in the stone quarry—they immediately invited us to supper after our arrival and asked if we wouldn't take all our meals together with the families. We shared our food equally with them; the women helped us store our equipment and in the evenings we spent in lively conversation, as much as we were able. There was a thorough human demeanor on their side that did us good. They did not in the least see us, as was known everywhere else, that we were the enemies of their country. Every now and again one heard the sorrowful expression: "*Oui, c'est la guerre.*"

He also expresses deep sorrow and sympathy for a civilian who hangs himself when a town is reoccupied by the Germans: "In his pocket was found a paper upon which it was written: 'Two times the German soldiers have stolen my possessions; I will not live through a third.'" This indicates a level of civility and empathy that was not to be repeated two decades later during the next world war.

Even French soldiers are viewed in Artur's eyes as human beings. When he takes a prisoner during one battle, he demands that his opponent furnish him with water to quench his thirst, but the Frenchman holds up an empty canteen, and Artur feels remorse for one who had been "thirsty even longer than I."

The British, on the other hand, seem rather more inscrutable to Artur. He notes that their aviators, while brave, were often foolhardy. In one battle, clearly outmaneuvered, an English aviator is eventually forced to earth with a mortal wound, but the tenacity of his fighting elicits admiration from Artur and his compatriots on the ground. In another instance, a fierce battle with the English involves their enemy bombarding them not with shells, but rather with garbage, which the Germans feel is belittling of fellow soldiers, especially since the trenches were only about thirty feet (ten meters) apart. As he states: "This mischief went on for a time until the Bavarians, who no longer wanted to participate in the joke any further, one fine day took off their tunics, tucked up their shirttails, and each man armed himself with a cudgel. Then and there they sprang out of the trenches, ran on over to the enemy, gave them a good thrashing in their trenches." He also reports that after a fierce battle, a captured English commander attempted to congratulate the victorious Bavarians as "to thank them for a good match." The reaction, a slap upside the head by a Bavarian soldier, made it clear that, given the deaths on both sides, this sort of "sport" was unappreciated.

In late 1917 Artur encounters for the first time American doughboys. America, which had entered the war formally only in April, was long neutral, though a number of volunteers fought with the allied forces. According to him, his first encounters with them were on the Noyon–Mont Didier Front, when a few were captured following an unsuccessful charge.[5] He states: "As usual, we tried to engage in a trade exchange with smoked meats for food or other goods that the enemy had in abundance. As we attempted to speak English with them, they answered in German: 'Speak German with us, for we know the language.' It emerged that these young men came from German families in America, and they enlisted in the service after they had become Americans." This was startling, for it is clear that Artur did not expect to find linguistically

Introduction

compatible soldiers among these recent troops. He was certainly unaware that his simple statement underlined difficulties that German-American families had back in the United States with their heritage.[6] This is the only real confrontation with Americans; despite the title of the chapter, Artur only sees the changes in tactics, mainly from the air, that dissolve the stalemate once they arrive and engage in the war.

The Russians, French, English and Americans were not the only enemies that the Germans fought in World War I. He also encountered non–European troops. As Christian Koller notes: "In the First World War more than 600,000 non-white soldiers from the French and British colonies fought in the European theatre of war, among them 270,000 Maghrebins, 153,000 Indians and 134,000 West Africans."[7] During his second stay on the Meuse-Argonne Front, he mentions the strength of the French "colonial" or "colored" soldiers: "At this particular front the French had mingled their attack strength with troops from the colonies, and one was never certain about a night attack." He explains further:

> It was already known to us that the enemy used colored soldiers for defense back in 1914, when the Germans made their surprise advance almost to Paris. At that time fighting was sometimes almost like jungle warfare. The harvest was fully underway in France, and there where the troops advanced across the fields the reaping was already finished and the sheaves erected. During the night the front was guarded with patrols during the offensive. But all too often it seemed that many people went missing. We didn't want to or would not believe that they had been taken prisoner by the enemy, for there was no sound of fighting. But soon soldiers with their throats slit were found everywhere among the standing sheaves of wheat. It was an insidious war. The colonial soldiers, often black as night in color, hid in the sheaves and acted according to their customs from their wild homelands with only knives as an effective weapon.

Most likely Artur fought West Africans from the French colonies, as Richard Fogarty explains:

> As they did when recruiting soldiers from the colonies, officers made distinctions between *races guerrières and races non-guerrières*. The latter, such as Indochinese and Madagascans, often found themselves relegated to non-combat duty, laboring as *troupes d'étapes*, or staging troops. Their allegedly more warlike compatriots, most West Africans and North Africans, served in combat at the front.... Members of "races" that French officers considered particularly warlike and aggressive found themselves used almost exclusively in the attack as *troupes de choc*, or shock troops, which, of course, increased their chances of injury or death in comparison with members of supposedly less warlike races. Nonetheless many French officers questioned the suitability of even supposedly warlike

indigènes for use in European warfare, revealing the durability of assumptions about the inferiority of nonwhites.⁸

In Germany, this prewar image of foreign colonial soldiers sometimes even went so far as to represent them as feral animals. The German Foreign Office put out a memorandum entitled "Employment, contrary to International Law, of Colored Troops upon the European Theatre of War by England and France" in 1915, in which "many atrocities were attributed to colonial soldiers, namely the poking out of eyes and the cutting off ears, noses and heads of wounded and captured German soldiers," according to Christian Koller.⁹

From his description, Artur too follows this contemporary view noted by Fogarty and Koller, noting that the colonials conducted themselves in battle with similar atrocities. But he also displays a good measure of fear, particularly since the subtext is that such "jungle warfare" is antithetical to European civilized military conduct. Nonetheless, he feels that these "uncivilized" soldiers were still due respect and the Germans had the obligation to treat these troops with the same decorum when captured.

A few pages later Artur relates a battle fought on the Champagne Front near the city of Reims between these black soldiers and the Bavarian troops. He is obviously shocked and displeased with the vicious and brutal outcome of that battle:

> After a hard battle they succeeded in driving back the enemy, but afterwards the city itself had to be cleansed of the remaining French. This led to one of the most difficult actions during the World War. If the troops as a whole could report good success, the Bavarians lost a huge strength of their own in the cleansing. And the most tragic part of it was that the soldiers were attacked by the black troops and many were murdered from behind. The bitterness was limitless concerning this, and when at last the enemy was overcome, the Bavarians took no black prisoners, but rather shot every single Negro.

Like many a soldier Artur shared many experiences, good and bad, with enemy civilians and soldiers. The good experiences gave him back faith in man's humanity and the bad confirmed the worst of mankind's treatment. The enemy, however similar or different, is still reckoned as compatriots in arms, and as such is due respect and perhaps even admiration at times, no matter how horrific or terrifying the battles. Artur Boer was completely capable of distinguishing between the human and the inhuman in his memoir.

Introduction

War is, however, not just the confrontation between enemies, but rather each soldier was allotted a specific duty or task that served to make the war function, whether among a group of people who were to advance the lines or those whose logistical support was crucial towards the attainment of the goals of the military.

Life as a Sapper

Artur Boer's main function as a soldier was as a combat engineer or sapper, as noted previously. His regiment, whose home base was in Stettin, consisted mainly of engineering companies supporting the various combat units. Artur was assigned to the group which was responsible for the logistics required in the field and for military assaults, the "*Pioneers.*"[10] He was tasked with digging and maintaining trenches, bunkers, foxholes, and other positions, in addition to laying and repairing barbed wire, handling munitions, monitoring depots, laying communication or telephone wires, and later building "tank traps." They were all-armed combat troops but were rarely required to engage in direct fighting, though it is clear that there is a grey area here between their normal functions and combat that was crossed repeatedly. Unlike regular infantry, however, they did not participate in the numerous, often futile charges towards the enemy trenches, though there were occasions that required them to tag along, or to be working in between the regular engagements.

Immediately upon arrival at the unidentified location on the Eastern Front, Artur paints a vivid picture of a sapper's life:

> As a pioneer company we always had our main camp headquarters about eight kilometers back of our own lines. According to the organization, this was intended to be a perquisite that was shown us as one of the top companies. The object was to minimize our losses as much as possible during the stalemate at the front. But one of the inevitable inconveniences was that we had to traverse a roadless and trackless Russia. Each evening before twilight we had to undergo a two or three hours march to the front laden with tools, building supplies, ammunition, and barbed wire. If met with a withering Russian fire that landed immediately behind the front, we could hardly clear the stretch with caution and stealth in four hours. As soon as we arrived we were allowed a ten minute pause and then divided up into groups and sent into no-man's land to dig trenches or lay and repair the barbed wire fences. It was obvious that we came under fire from the enemy suddenly and without warning, for the two sides were no more

than fifty meters from each other. So there was nothing to do but to duck as quickly as possible with one's head to the ground, or to dive into some shell crater. We soon became so trained at this that the moves were instinctive; thus our losses in these circumstantial attacks were thankfully minimal. But it was worse to work so close when the enemy used flares. For many minutes the field of battle was illuminated, and the machine guns of the enemy used the opportunity to pepper any object there.... It was not enough that our work was tense and dangerous in no-man's land. We soon had quotas to fulfill; i.e., each group was required to complete a certain number of meters of barbed wire fence.... I have always wanted to meet the person who could tie the so-called Spanish riders made of barbed wire in the dark without injuring himself!

Despite being quartered behind the active front, much of Artur's descriptions involve doing his job under duress, being targeted directly as they struggled to meet these "quotas," generally set by commanding officers with little or no experience in the dangers of the front. Here on the Eastern Front, their main job was to encroach upon no man's land with new positions or trenches, fortifying them with barbed wire to prevent the Russians from successful charges. As such, it was work that was exposed and dangerous, as he notes often in the memoirs. This required that the sappers had to work quickly, especially with particular defensive materials like the Spanish riders, or *Chevel de Frise*. These were like knife holders with barbed wire which were designed to slow the progress of an attack, and it is clear that the sappers were expected to create these on the spot, no easy task. The other engineering works were of a more limited nature on this front; the digging of redoubts, the repairs to the same, and the transporting of ammunition.

Life on the Western Front was more technical and complex, for it required an entirely different set of skills, even though the basic tasks were the same. There the variety of duties of the sappers were multiplied considerably from what they had been in the east. Not only was the terrain different and more variable than the forests, the give and take of the battles, or rather, skirmishes during the stalemate meant that their work took on new and sometimes far more dangerous dimensions. Moreover, their duties sometimes went far beyond those expected of a pioneer. As Artur himself stated: "We were there primarily to do manual labor." This meant more or less menial tasks, which needed to be done in addition to their normal jobs.

Throughout the time Artur spent on the front lines in France, a greater portion of it was spent actually in the trenches themselves

Introduction

rather than behind the front. He noted his first duties involved some similar tasks like those done in the east, though in a more troglodyte manner:

> In the front trenches themselves there was a bunker every ten meters, dug into the earth until there was about four or five meters of covering above. Down there in the depths all of these rooms were connected so that there was the possibility of saving the soldiers in the case one of the rooms received a direct hit and was demolished. These connections were the most important task that we had to do. On the other hand, during the night hours we worked in no man's land to renew and expand the barbed wire to secure the positions.

The activity meant that he and his company were required to spend long periods of time in the bunkers themselves, for their duties were to be done both day and night. There were, of course, times when the company was able to march back to bivouacs behind the front, but as time went on, these became more sporadic, and conditions in the trenches that Artur describes become more and more terrible.

The primary duties included the excavation of the trenches themselves, particularly after they and the bunkers they contained collapsed due to enemy shelling. These positions were also those starting points from which the pioneers dug underground in the hopes of mining or undermining the nearby trenches of the enemy. His view of the safety of the trenches can be seen in this anecdote:

> If underneath the ground we felt ourselves safe from bullets and shells, we were not always certain that we were without peril. It happened in our company one time that, during a short pause in our work, we heard tapping in the ground from the enemy side. Of course, it was only natural that the opponents were doing the same sort of work against our positions. Our observations were reported and we were told to break off the job. Instead, we mounted a microphone in the tunnel with a wire leading up to the trenches. Now we listened the entire time and determined that the enemy really was at work in our proximity. This was heard for a long time by a guard post, but suddenly all sound ceased. Two of our boys now received orders to investigate the situation carefully and see what happened to the microphone. When too much time had passed for the return of the boys, a couple of others went down into the shaft. These soon came back and said that the first group must have fainted due to the gas that lay in a pool at the bottom of the hole. We suspected that the enemy knew how close we were. They had broken through and taken the microphone, and then filled the tunnel with carbon dioxide gas. Several men equipped with gas masks fetched the boys, and they immediately were put in the care of doctors and taken to the hospital. The shaft was immediately filled with explosives and detonated.

In their attempts to gain advantage over the enemy, they had to contend with the dangers inherent in mines: lack of ventilation, build-ups of toxic gas, and the fear of discovery.

In another area, his company was involved in constructing a short mine railway that was narrow gauge and consisted of wagons that could be hauled up an incline by animals or rope with supplies and ammunition, and then returned by way of gravity, with the guiding ropes acting as brakes. He often describes the need to repair this transportation method, which involved gang work more common to railway workers.

Not all his efforts on the Western Front were devoted to manual labor, and there are instances of his entire sapper company doing their normal duty of stringing telephone lines back to the command headquarters or building pontoon bridges, work for which they had been trained. On the Meuse-Argonne Front, they also planted explosives, and in one story, Artur and his company succeed in wiring dynamite to some ruins just in time to detonate it as a charge by colonial soldiers is underway. At this stage, they immediately go from being engineers to regular combat troops repelling the enemy successfully. As he notes: "The next instant we heard and saw a huge detonation among the ruins. We had successfully connected the electricity to the explosive wires. The mission had succeeded. But the boys had observed and by now we too understood that the enemy was coming. And these were not just a few, but rather at least an entire company. Luckily, we were all at our posts and could meet the charge with our warmest response." Life as a sapper truly required not only the technical skills to be able to fulfill the engineering needs of the German army, they also needed to be combat-ready and to participate as ordinary soldiers in armed confrontations.

Whether out in the open and becoming moving targets to working underground, Artur's life stands in stark contrast to that of the German officers, those in command who planned and gave the orders.

Rank and Privilege

The rank and file often viewed officer corps with contempt that was called *Offiziershaß* (or the hate for officers) due to what Alexander Watson calls "a front-rear divide."[11] The German officers were a privileged rank with their stations set back from the front. In the Somme

Introduction

valley in 1916, the officer's quarters were "dugouts ... thirty to forty feet deep, connected by tunnels and steel railway systems. Electric lights and ventilation was provided in all rooms, and many of them had paneled walls and planked floors." Some were positively luxurious, replete with white-washed ceilings, varnished woodwork, carpets, and wallpaper.[12] Elsewhere further behind the front, officers commandeered larger estates for their headquarters, and most reveled in a lifestyle that included comfortable lodgings, ample supplies, and many perquisites that gave them all of the trappings of their higher rank.

As Artur describes this state of affairs, the differences between the officers and the ordinary soldier were stark and telling:

> The officers never had to eat anything like that which was doled out to us from the field kitchens. They had their own kitchens, and it was normal that one obtained for themselves a butcher as a cook. The military post or special procurement of extra rations and drink were sent far behind the front.
>
> On calmer fronts, an officer's mess was created where one could have the pleasant company of officers from other divisions. We often had the occasion to hear of these feasts while on guard duty. And when the circumstances were right, there were parties with other divisions. Musicians from the company who had their instruments with them were drafted for these occasions. Now, one didn't want to envy these gentlemen their pleasure, were it not for the fact that many times the food of the troops was limited or bad. We ourselves were content with what we had to live on, but only if it was enough. But sometimes it could be too much, and we noticed that the company cook attempted to hide from our view the extra provisions that we could have purchased from the various marketplaces. This was usually a matter of wine and the better smoked meats.

Indeed, sometimes even packages of food sent to the ordinary soldiers from their homes never made it. Leaves for rest and recreation were sporadic and difficult to come by for the troops, but the officers were allowed home leave several times a year, and for this purpose first- and second-class rail coaches were reserved. Some officers even lived normal lives as they might back in Germany, as Artur notes: "About three miles behind the front lines there were also French civilians, and for the officers who had their billets there, there was a possibility of living a life no garrison in Germany could offer: cinemas, theaters, and sporting arenas, and, moreover, in the cities were to be found hotels and bordellos that were only visited by the officers."

This, needless to say, engendered a love-hate relationship with the officer class, where on one hand military discipline required that these commanders be given the utmost respect and privilege for their rank, and on the other the discontent among the lower ranks fomented by the officers' excesses which stood in stark contrast to the often miserable circumstances of the troops under their command. Artur is not unequivocal in his view of this contrast. The most evident case can be found in several passages concerning a platoon commander by the name of Lieutenant Küsters.[13] He first appears in the memoir during the battle at the Bois de Caillette:

> At twelve at night one of our platoon commanders, Lieutenant Küsters, arrived to lead us soldiers back. He stopped next to me and said, "How on earth are we going to get back through all that withering fire?" We turned around and noticed that there were shell craters in the earth all about, just like drops of rain on a flat surface. "Where are our boys? I can't find them." I made him aware that our "boys" had to be sought along that stretch. We then decided that everyone would gather at the craters and advance. But after an hour we could bring no more than nine men and two captured French soldiers, who begged us to take them behind our lines.
>
> We all moved out. It was a singing and resounding hell. It was pitch black night, and the shells flashed across us. Shrapnel whined about our ears. There seemed to be only a slim chance in a thousand to get through with a whole skin. We jumped, ran, fell into every little depression in the ground so that we would not be observed. The only thought that consoled us was that we were not separated from each other. I still to this day do not understand how we twelve men somehow gained the protection of our own walls.

Clearly, the lieutenant was sent out to rescue "his" men personally, which was one of the duties of front line officers. The German officers were trained in a so-called "aristocratic ethos," which "demanded that junior leaders look after their men's welfare and lead them by example into battle," according to Alexander Watson.[14] That being said, he relies upon Artur and his comrades to extricate themselves from their midnight predicament. In short, he had no clue as to how he was to accomplish his task, and as a result the survival of both his missing men and their French prisoners is due more to serendipity than his leadership. Implied but left unsaid by Artur is that only those on the front lines knew how to deal with the situation.

Then, when he arrives for the second time on the Meuse-Argonne Front, Artur describes this officer once again in two contrasting scenarios, first as a true leader in the aristocratic ethos sense, and the second as a crass incompetent. In the first, he sees the miserable rations that his troops are eating and decides to share his officer-class sandwiches with them. Artur describes this incident:

Introduction

> This officer was the most zealous person possible, who demanded the utmost possible from his personnel, both in terms of work and battle. For him, nothing was impossible. But he never spared himself, whatever task lay before him. On a day patrol with a few men to seek out a new path towards the front, a pause was called in order to eat a bite of food. We took out our bread and spread on it some thin marmalade. He too took out his packet of sandwiches that his adjutant had made for him. On his sandwiches there was, apart from good butter, various tasty morsels. When he saw how meager our bread with marmalade was in comparison with his, he became angry. He divided his sandwich in pieces, and we gave him some of ours. Upon the return to the camp he sought out his adjutant and this man had to serve in the company for a week as punishment. Likewise, he quite seldom partook of the succulent offerings that the cook provided his officers.

Artur's description of Küsters as "zealous" is kindly meant here, for he describes the officer's diligence and focus, but at the same time provides evidence that he was concerned with their welfare to the point of sharing his own specially-prepared food. His connection with his men is implied as close enough that he eschews the normal privilege of the officer class in the matter of rations. He is, however, not entirely comradely, for at the same time he apparently blames his adjutant for the disparity in rations, forcing this unwitting aide-de-camp to undergo punishment.

In terms of the second description as an incompetent leader, a short time thereafter he gives an absurdly ridiculous order only to have to rescind it, which is the very antithesis of his role in leadership:

> On another occasion we were to lie in reserve in a trench in back of the first front line. This was also under the command of Küsters. Right in front of us was a hill so that we had no line of sight towards the front lines. There the battle raged intensely, but we were shelled heavily by rifle bullets that dropped down on us. The post was dug in such short proximity in order to give the alarm when the danger of a breakthrough was imminent. Of course, the people stationed there sought shelter behind the breastworks against the shells. Lieutenant Küsters observed this and ordered that the soldiers should stand upright with half their bodies unprotected against the enemy, even though a view forward was impossible because of the hill. The lieutenant's order was issued with the threat that he would immediately shoot anyone who hid behind the shield. Those posted there nonetheless knew when we would become involved, for the eventual retreating forces there would have become visible in enough time. But at the orders of the officer, all of a sudden the respect completely collapsed, and an old solider went up to the lieutenant saying: "Shoot, shoot as many as you can, for the faster you do, the faster the war is over for us."

The notion that one should show bravado and expose themselves to be killed is stupidity of the highest order, and the troops knew it. The old soldier's retort that their leader ought to go ahead and shoot his own men to shorten the war is equally absurd, but the point was well-taken at this juncture. Artur dryly notes: "The lieutenant certainly understood the idiocy of the order and repealed it."

The final anecdote concerning Küsters appears as the war is ending, and he is wounded. Here, the sense of duality is prevalent, with the lieutenant being portrayed as still concerned with his rank and duties, even though he has lost the respect of the men under his command:

> At the very end we had the last losses to note: three dead and five wounded. Among the latter was Lieutenant Küsters. He received a nasty bullet wound in the calf, and we carried him to the ambulance. His last words to us were: "What will happen to the company when I am no longer with them?" We who heard them could only smile in answer. His zealousness and huge belief in himself could not be suppressed, even though he lay on a stretcher. Long afterwards we learned moreover that he had his leg amputated at the hospital. His faith as a soldier must finally have been little more than a joke by then.

Lieutenant Küsters was not the only officer Artur considered arrogant. Earlier he reports a surprise inspection by an unnamed lieutenant that is not entirely up to the stolid officer's expectations:

> This leader, a first lieutenant, was standing about a hundred meters from the company but still observed movement in our ranks. He went directly to me and asked me if I hadn't understood the command. I thought, "You really are stupid," but I remained silent. He put the same question to my comrade next to me. He remained silent as well. "Both of you will do one hour on report," came his order.

Fortunately, in this instance the corporal assigned to oversee the punishment realizes that both soldiers are well-disciplined veterans and allows them to complete it without stress.

Artur's view of the officer class doesn't actually resonate with a deeper sense of *Offizierhaß,* but there is an undercurrent that shows that his views may have been suppressed in the memoir, and that he was no less derogatory about rank and privilege than other common soldiers.

This can be seen in his description of the military newspapers that circulated among the trenches, which were used, as they are today, largely as positive propaganda pieces. After the first battle at Verdun in 1916, initially portrayed as a German victory at a horrendous cost of almost three quarters of a million casualties on both sides, German Crown Prince Friedrich Wilhelm (1882–1951) was portrayed in the press as a German hero, despite his early assertions on the war itself and his stepping down as supreme German commander in November after the tide of battle changed.[15] The memoir contains an anecdote wherein the paper showed a picture of the Crown Prince with "enthusiastic" soldiers running after his car as it went by an unidentified camp. The reality of this scene is described as a stage prop, wherein the soldiers were told to line up with the inducement of extra rations, and the picture was snapped as the Prince's adjutant threw (or was about to throw) handfuls of cigarettes to the assembled troops. It was apparent that even to those not in attendance, this propaganda picture was a bogus attempt at morale boosting and that the "Butcher of Verdun," as the Crown Prince was known, had little following among his subjects. In short, As Artur notes: "The effect on us was that this paper had about the same veracity as the tale of the stork for a half-grown child." Or, as he puts it another way: "The comradery between higher officers and soldiers therein was mostly pure fiction."

The disparity of rank and privilege was palpable. For the ordinary German soldier in action, Artur frequently notes that reliance was not to be made on their leadership, but rather on the weapons of war, upon which their survival depended.

Weaponry

World War I saw the beginning of the change to modern warfare, including the dawn of the so-called weapons of mass destruction. As Ann Linder states, this was "the shape of things to come—a world in which the revered cavalry and its cherished horses were anachronisms, the despised engineers were indispensable, and the inglorious machine, in the form of the high explosive shell and the machine gun, was the real lord of the battlefield."[16] Throughout the memoir, showers of shells and bullets are ubiquitous, and Artur frequently mentions the devastating effects in terms of casualties and devastation. In his duties as a sapper, he often came under fire, and the descriptions of this include sounds like the "buzzing of bees" and the scattering of shrapnel around him like rain. Indeed, a large portion of the memoir has the continuous sound of shelling in the background, with equal barrages of bullets, either from machine guns or rifles, all around him as he works. Despite this extremely dangerous environment, Artur does begin to express a certain nonchalance about the enemy's firepower, occasionally even noting that he didn't worry about dangers over much. This did not mean, however, that the constant sight of the seriously wounded, dead, and dying, not to mention the various dismembered corpses, didn't bother him. In one instance on the Eastern Front, he is forced to shoot from behind a dead Russian soldier, and he gives a poignant glimpse into a scene he found disturbing: "In the high grass right in front of me I discovered a dead Russian; the passing of each of my bullets lifted his long, blond hair and a scrap of his open shirt." That this sight should disturb him indicates that he was not immune to the constant horror.

As far as his own armaments were concerned, as a sapper he generally carried little beyond the normal equipment of a soldier. As his photograph in Chapter 1 shows, this is a large grenade and a rifle, both of which he mentions using while at the front. The former came in two types, a more common barrel shape called a *"Stielhandgrenate"* or stick grenade (as seen in the illustration), and the so-called *"Eierhandgranate,"* or egg grenade, a compact device that could be thrown up to 50 yards. There were, of course, other sorts, but these are the two specifically identified by Artur.

In terms of larger field guns, he generally refers to them generically as artillery without specification, largely because they were fired by other companies than his. He is concerned with both the saturation shelling and retaliatory shelling on both fronts, but only as to how it relates to his own work as a sapper and not due to any fascination regarding types or development. There are, of course, exceptions.

During his time on the Eastern Front, he notes first barrages by what he calls "20 cm/s" howitzers, either the 21 cm Mörser 10 or 10.5 cm *leichte Feldhaubitze* 98/09, though his description of them being directed against machine gun nests would seem to indicate the smaller of the two cannon. Later, in anticipation of the storming of the fortress at Rózan, he states that the German army brings up the 30.5 cm howitzers, also known as *Schlanke Emma*. These were significant siege guns of large caliber that could fire the so-called *Granatschrapnell* shell of 385 kilograms which was mainly used against entrenched infantry. These were developed in Austria but widely used throughout the theatres of war. On the Western Front, he also indicates the 15 cm howitzer, a Model 18 *schwere Feldhaubitze* which was used, ineffectually, as an anti-aircraft gun. Finally, towards the end of the memoir Artur

Introduction

makes reference to the most terrifying weapon of all: "In September-October of 1918 the Germans had constructed a cannon that could shell Paris, a distance of twelve miles." This was the so-called *Lange Max* (also called *Big Bertha*), which could fire a shell 70 miles (12 German miles or 120 kilometers). An inaccurate weapon of terror, this cannon was of little strategic importance, and Artur appears only to have heard about it, not seen it.

Bruce Gudmundsson notes: "Heavy artillery, including heavy field howitzers, was not made a permanent part of most German divisions until late in 1917. From the very beginning of the war, however, each passing month saw more heavy artillery made available for temporary attachment to German divisions."[17] It would seem from their constant use by the German army on both fronts described in the memoir that there may have been more than just "temporary attachments," as the requirements for the shelling of enemy positions in advance of the constant attacks, even during the stalemate, were omnipresent.

Other weapons of war of a more novel nature also appear in the memoir. These include three that were to significantly change the very nature of the battle: tanks, air power, flame throwers, and poison gas.

In the autumn of 1915 Artur goes to the Western Front where he encounters tanks or "rolling fortresses":

> We only waited for the traveling marvel to come a bit closer. We had only a vague idea how to fight these tanks effectively when they came in range. We could of course use our anti-tank weapons industriously, but these heavy weapons could only be loaded with one shell at a time, and therefore we had to make every shot count. Machine guns were of no use whatsoever against an attacking tank.

These early tanks, the first use of which was at the Battle of the Somme in September of 1916, were first fielded by the British troops. The one used in this battle was the Mark I, which was soon replaced by French Schneider CA and Char Saint Charmond models. In his chapter entitled "French Tank Attack," it seems like the latter was the type that Artur's company encountered. By this time in 1918 the Germans had developed the *Geballte Ladung* ("bunched charge"), a shell that could penetrate the heavy armor of this vehicle, though, as he notes, firing it was problematic: "This was almost three times larger than the usual weapon, and the ammunition was much bigger and made of steel instead of the usual lead used by the normal projectiles. The striking strength was calculated to pierce eight millimeters of tank armor. Apart from the size, this weapon was difficult to handle." On the other hand, given that these vehicles were so slow and cumbersome, he and his sapper company were able to construct barriers, or "tank traps," that rendered this new threat ineffective.

The new weapons of warfare were the airplanes. These replaced balloons as useful tools for reconnaissance and observation of the enemy. Balloons had been a part of the military arsenal for a half a century by the start of the First World War, but their combat capabilities were limited. As noted in *A Multimedia History of World War I*:

> Observation balloons were commonly adopted by all sides and considered ideal in the static trench warfare conditions largely peculiar to the First World War.... Observation readings were passed down via the use of flags or occasionally by radio, and balloon operators would generally remain in the air for hours at a spell. It was regarded as a dangerous job, for although observation balloons were invariably heavily protected by anti-aircraft and machine gun fire and by wire meshes dangled between groups of balloons, they were often the irresistible stationary target of enemy aircraft.[18]

Artur does not mention the larger, mobile balloons, the dreaded Zeppelins, though he must have been aware of them. He does mark their existence, however. During the stalemate in Champagne, he states: "Both French and German observation balloons were up both day and night observing every movement around and in back of both fronts." Later, he gets more descriptive about what these looked like, commenting: "Observations were done by airplane reconnaissance and the long sausage-like observation balloons, which were up in the air day and night."

During the Argonne campaign, however, he notes some further specifics about balloons and how they were used and guarded:

> We positioned our observations balloons about one or two miles behind the battle trenches. These waived like large sausages at a height of about two hundred meters and were fastened by means of steel cables to a machine that regulated their position in the air, as well as raising and lowering them on the command of the observer. In the beginning, many were shot down by the enemy's pilots. The reason was that the machinery functioned too slowly or that there were not enough defenses on the ground. In these cases, the occupant jumped down with a parachute. But later we mounted fast-firing so-called flak guns (anti-aircraft cannon) whose every tenth shell was filled with magnesium, and new orders for raising and lowering the balloon were given, making it difficult for the enemy to come close to these important observation posts.

Introduction

Here he is aware that it was the airplane, not the balloon that was the main ruler of the sky in time of war.

His main interest was as an observer on the ground, watching the aerial arabesques of the planes above. He describes the general function of these new weapons, which at first were to watch enemy movements, spot artillery, take photographs, and signal ground troops with rockets and drop messages to their ground troops. Later pilots became combatants as well, taking over the Zeppelin mission of dropping bombs and later attacking both air and ground targets with mounted guns. In several passages the reader can ascertain the role of the airplane in the war:

> A French aviator flew over us. This meant that we had to be absolutely still in order not to betray our new position. But it was not long afterwards that small bore shells began to whistle overhead. The opposition had still not correctly deduced our position, and we had to begin to build new defensive trenches immediately. The soldier who had gone for water returned and we drank ourselves to satisfaction for the first time in a long while. Immediately, several other soldiers went out after water, but they returned momentarily. A young infantryman handed back our canteens and with horror in his eyes only pointed to the place from which he had returned. The air was filled with shrapnel, and many corpses lay about the wagon. High overhead an aviator circled, leading the enemy fire to the wagon.

Posted to the front just north of Champagne, a corporal and Artur are assigned to a depot to distribute ammunitions. Both men express their concern that the depot might be seen by "an aviator." A depot is indeed discovered just south of their position, and a squadron of planes commences an aerial attack:

> We crept out of the protective bunker and saw that the bombers had succeeded in setting the ammunition depot to the south of us on fire. This was the grandest fireworks that the enemy had yet incurred. The explosions, each stronger than the next, were an exciting theatrical play. Sky high fire fountains lit up the heavens. We later learned that the bombed depot had received three trains filled with ammunition from Germany. We heard detonations from that bombing for several days thereafter. Such a firestorm can never be extinguished.

Thereafter, descriptions of bombing raids are not uncommon, and Artur notes that the troops on the ground can even distinguish between the sounds of German and Allied airplane engines.

His most engaging descriptions of these new weapons involve the aerial combats, the dogfights that are undertaken in the skies as the ground troops watch from below, much as one might watch a sporting match. Near the Bapaume Front, Artur is close to the airfields used by German ace Baron von Richthofen. It is evident that Artur is aware of the "Red Baron" by the color of his airplane, a Fokker Triplane. Indeed, Richthofen's squadron was easily followed by the troops on the ground because of their colorfully painted airplanes, which earn them the nickname "the Flying Circus."[19] Roger Chickering writes:

> Images of individual heroism survived only in the sky, in the figures of aviators like Willi Boelcke and Manfred von Richthofen, whose celebrity was the issue of a wedding between modern aerial technology and medieval forms of combat, which themselves soon receded into the anonymity of squadron tactics. Heroic images had no relevance, however, for the masses of the foot soldiers, who were more aptly portrayed as the proletarians of industrial war, or as animals that burrowed into muddy labyrinths for shelter until they emerged—in what were called offensives—to offer pale challenge to the modern machines that ruled the battlefield and blocked access to enemy trenches.[20]

Artur has several encounters with aerial combat, beginning on the Eastern Front. During the siege of the Kreuzburg, he notices the first battles above in the sky:

> After a time we saw the first of the Russian air battles up in the sky. Their Russian airplanes were constructed with more armor compared with ours, and thus it was difficult to damage them from the ground. We were convinced that, if the Russians had had many of this sort of plane, our offensive would have been impossible to carry out. These planes flew easily and undisturbed at an altitude 500 meters above us, taking no notice of our anti-aircraft batteries, which weren't as effective as they would become later on in the war.

The actual scene is contradictory; for he notes that these are "battles" and yet the remainder of the observation leads one to believe that the Russian aircraft were merely observers of the action below. Such is not the case, however, with his descriptions of dogfights on the Western Front.

Sighting these became an everyday event for Artur, and he watched the tactics employed by Richthofen in his duels:

> From the earliest time of the morning until late at night there was a terrible activity in the skies above us. Our eyes were directed upwards towards the firmament, whatever time of day it was. If one heard machine gun patter, one looked up first and foremost at the smaller cloud formations. The Red Baron kept himself hidden in back of these in order to swoop like a hawk on the opposition. Richthofen showed a singular cold-bloodedness, but in every battle that we observers saw, the English aviators were brave and refused to give in until the very last. But it was Richthofen and his men who most often won with their battle tactics.

Introduction

He also noted that the various aviators, German and Allied, were identifiable by their manner of combat. He states that the English were stubborn and refuse to give in, while the German opponents were often ruthless and relentless in their battle tactics. Even so, a certain esprit de corps could be seen; he notes that if a single Allied airplane came across a squadron of German planes, only one of the latter would engage in a dogfight. Later, he describes an English plane that seems oblivious to the danger: "But then we discovered two large German biplanes at a fortuitous height. If the Englishman was interested in what he saw or if stupidity simply took over, he nonchalantly ignored these large machines and circled continuously above us at a great height." In another instance, a dogfight, the Englishman is mortally wounded but manages to land his plane near the trenches. The German pilot, a major from Würtemmberg, immediately lands beside the wreck and takes charge of the Englishman's identification and effects, a chivalrous act to a worthy but defeated enemy.

Despite the rather detailed descriptions of the air war, the actual mention of types of aircraft is virtually non-existent. Only once does Artur mention a specific one, a Rumpler, though he does not tell which model it is.

Perhaps the most terrifying weapon that appears in the memoir is gas, used by both sides. As Al Mauroni notes:

> At the beginning of World War I, no nation was actively seeking a chemical warfare capability, although some scientists and military analysts had suggested the possibility. The decision to employ gas munitions came as a result of deadlock caused by trench warfare. As the two sides hunkered down, gaining ground became very difficult and very expensive in terms of human lives, resources, and time.... Although the Germans retained a technological lead over the British and French throughout the war, all three nations invested heavily in this new form of warfare. At this point in history, chemical weapons were not considered "weapons of mass destruction," but they did play a significant role as tactical weapons.[21]

The use of carbon dioxide has already been mentioned, but far more deadly gases, such as chlorine and mustard gas, were used, often with devastating effect. Given that these had to be dispersed through hollow artillery shells or by prevailing winds, the dangers of a gas attack would be great for both attacker and the target. In one scene at the Chemins des Dames, Artur's company is issued a gas mask with filters, which was to be kept at hand all the time. They are to go out in the wake of an attack and prepare new positions. In crossing the front they discovered its effects, as he states:

> Everywhere, on the roads, in the trenches, in the bunker we found masses of dead. But all of these corpses showed an unpleasant color in their faces and hands. There weren't many that were buried by shells, but rather all we could see were those poisoned by German gas. We were forced to put on our gas masks to protect ourselves from our own gas that was left in the area. We were forbidden to sit down, for the gas still remained in the knee-high grass. We were also strictly admonished not to touch any of the enemy's food, which we would otherwise have gladly confiscated. Everything was poisoned.

As he writes in his own preface, the worst thing that soldiers encountered was gas, and throughout the memoir he often skirts the subject of its effects, though of course it is part of his continuous war narrative.[22] But whatever the deadly consequences of these attacks, both enemy and friendly, there was an effect upon the necessary sustenance required for life itself; the spoiling of scarce food supplies in an already dire situation.

Food, Water, Rations

Food and drink are the most basic necessities of human life, and in the memoir their availability and quality remains a central part of the narrative. The abundance of food, including rare items, for the officer class has already been noted, as has the special circumstance wherein those in command had their own cooks and adjutants whose jobs were to provide adequate and fresh food in comfort and quantity. The theme throughout this memoir is that the common soldier's access to food, and most importantly drink, specifically fresh water, was not always a sure thing. Although all companies had supply wagons, the vicissitudes of war often prevented adequate nourishment from reaching the troops, a circumstance that Artur frequently notes.

This was not entirely the fault of the German military, whatever one might think of the disparity between the officers and common soldiers on the front. In August of 1914, shortly after the declaration of war, the British established a blockade of Germany, intending to cut off central Europe from receiving any supplies from overseas.[23] This included foodstuffs, which were deemed "contraband of war," and maritime commerce diminished considerably. When coupled with economic and climatic events in Germany, this meant that food as a commodity was often in short supply. Indeed, by the end of 1916 it had become critical. Linder notes:

> But as the Allied blockade of German ports tightened, imports ceased, and shortages appeared in 1915. By 1916 they were severe. In Germany, food was rationed, but even the legal ration was often unobtainable. Profiteering and black-marketing were rampant, rousing anger in civilian and soldier alike. The situation worsened with the crop failures of 1916 and the breakdowns in the transportation system. The bitterly cold winter of 1916–1917 was called the "Turnip Winter" because there was little other than turnips to eat.... The food situation did not markedly improve until the blockade was lifted in July of 1919 by which time an estimated 800,000 people had died of starvation and related diseases.[24]

Linder also comments on the rations of the German army noting that due to the Allied blockade, German troops were, after the first year of the war, very badly fed. That was particularly true in active sectors or during offensives, as rations had to be fetched at field kitchens well behind the front lines and hand-carried to the troops. During heavy shelling the rations and the ration carrier often failed to reach the troops.[25] Such circumstances are amply described throughout the memoir, as scrounging for food to supplement meager rations became almost an obsession.

In several instances, temporary truces between the opposing forces are arranged so that trade in foodstuffs could be made. For example, Artur notes that during one of these on the Eastern Front, alcohol and tobacco were exchanged for "eggs, butter, and meat," items which were in short supply. In his first meeting with Americans in 1918 he and his company also sought to barter for food. The majority of the time, however, his company was dependent upon the mess wagons, which were often detained behind the lines, forcing the troops to make do with limited food or forage for themselves.

Upon his return from the Eastern Front in July 1915 after recuperating from a wound, Artur's division marches to the front to conduct road maintenance and build bridges. As they advance against the enemy, he notes that the Russians set fire to everything so that nothing is left of crops or villages for the German soldiers. Artur calls this a scorched earth policy and the overall situation of providing the troops with adequate rations a "black chapter in military life." Just before he is wounded he notes that they were lucky to find a garden with apples and carrots to supplement their meager food. He states: "There was hardly any food to be found near the front. The depot was so emptied of useable food that our supply officers had been able to find only dried fish and vegetables for weeks. A loaf of bread was divided between four men, one hundred grams per man per day." Theft was the order of the day, either active raiding of Polish potato fields, or, if caught, through the dubious means of exchanging a worthless requisition scrip for the food taken.

That is not to say that the troops were always on such meager rations. After being wounded by a cluster shell, Artur "wolfed down" a hot meal of pork and peas, his first real food in a week and the last he was to have on the Eastern Front. While being transported to a hospital he describes even better rations: "We immediately received warm milk and thick, wonderful sandwiches, which we eagerly wolfed down." Later, during his recuperation at Wernigerode, the meals were not only pleasant, but substantial as well. As he states: "We as patients took our meals three times a day in the dining room of the main building." Such a luxury was not a frequent event, for the deprivations continued as he was posted to the Western Front.

Indeed, one entire chapter entitled "We Do Not Live by Bread Alone" is devoted mainly to food. It was either feast or famine; on quiet fronts the food was scarce, but he notes that on active fronts the troops were "cared for with the best provisions. We were given enough bread and oil, even fine jams." These postings contrasted with the usual provisions, which consisted, as he states, of reconstituted dried vegetables and "old" beef, a kilogram of bread (shared among three men), ersatz coffee, potatoes every third day, and "brown cabbage soup." On one occasion, not even this meager allotment was available, and the troops were consoled by a field church service (see photograph in Chapter 12) in compensation for the unavailability of rations. Considering this situation, it is no wonder that Artur reports that the troops looted food wherever they found it.

At the Chemin des Dames they passed through French villages and appropriated the necessary food and drink, because they were never sure that they would have a field mess. After an attack they lived on bread and water, loathe to touch the provisions that had been contaminated by the gas released by the enemy. As starving as they are, when no field kitchen arrives they are resigned to their fate:

> At five o'clock in the morning we were awakened by the watch. A mess orderly had come with a message that if we wanted any food we had to hurry up and come. The mess wagon lay on a country road and had been hit by a shell. Ten

men took off with the cook to get food for us. They had to go a long way over difficult territory to get to the road while the enemy artillery did everything possible to prevent a movement on the ground. A horrible picture presented itself upon our arrival. The shell had landed between the mess wagon and the horses, which were shredded into hamburger. The orderly too was missing, apparently also exploded into small pieces. The cook sat wounded on the edge of the ditch and the mess wagon was tottering on only one wheel. The shrapnel had shredded the bottoms of the pots and the food was slowly dripping out of the mess wagon. Another orderly had positioned himself a bit behind the mess when the shell hit and so was able to save himself. Some of us took the wounded in hand while others attempted to save what could be saved of the food. Then the cook was handed over to the medics or other members of the company, and the mess wagon was tipped over into the ditch.

Securing potable water was always an issue, as well. The troops were constantly either looking for natural sources or waiting for the water wagon. At the Battle of the Bois de Caillette in 1916, an active engagement where, as noted, the food was more abundant for those placed in mortal danger, water became a major issue. Artur describes the dichotomy between food and drink:

Our asking for food was not as important as our demand for water or something else drinkable. Provisions, consisting of preserved meat, bread, chocolate, and coffee, were doled out. We received only one mug of coffee per man, but if we wished it, then there was brandy in abundance. We swore against the orders that were able to obtain spirits for us but not water. We saved the coffee in our canteens and took a slug of brandy. One always took advantage of the occasion.[26]

In another instance, Artur captures a French soldier and demands a drink from his canteen, only to discover to his mortification that the enemy is no more successful than the Germans in provisioning their troops with water. Not only did they suffer, but were in some cases came close to starvation and could not attend to difficult work. If normal sustenance was a problem, life in the trenches was also problematic in terms of sanitary conditions.

Disease and Medication

Artur devotes an entire chapter entitled "Dirt, Lice, and Clay" to physical conditions in the trenches, but his views on sanitation in terms of also caring for the sick and wounded can be found throughout the memoir. There were no facilities at all on the Eastern Front for cleanliness, and the miasma of the dirt and grime must have been overwhelming for the troops.

He had already discovered how hard it was to keep clean on the Russian Front, but, comparatively speaking, the French front was far worse. On the Western Front he notes that some soldiers didn't leave the trenches for six months due to a shortage of relief troops. This meant that they were required to live for an extended period of time in quarters that were damp, muddy, and without proper sanitary facilities other than an outhouse bunker. This in turn made an ideal environment for disease and pestilence. According to Jeffry Lockwood: "The two sides [were] bogged down in the grim conditions of trench warfare. The crowded, filthy conditions were ideal for lice, and infestation rates quickly soared to nearly 90%."[27] Vermin included rats (and presumably other rodents), mosquitos, and lice, all of which bore disease-causing bacteria. In a humorous anecdote, Artur explains that to live with this infestation, the troops made sport of it:

> The circumstance of not being able to wash regularly and not being able to change clothes caused us much discomfort. But the worst plague was the pests that assailed us. Down in the bunkers where soldiers, who didn't have guard or other duty, slept were always filled with half-naked men. By the light of the wax candles everyone knocked loose the lice from their undergarments. This was a daily procedure, as much as we today clean our fingernails. It was the only important task we had to do during our off duty hours. It was normal to pluck between thirty and forty of the buggers off our clothing each day. During this occupation we soon became real "louse philosophers," dividing the lice into different classes. We learned their customs, their methods of creeping onto the body. We reported our daily catches to each other in wild and humor-filled news briefs. We sorted them by color and size into English, French, and Russians. The last were those that were the most dangerous of them because their bites were the worst, though small. We gathered them from among the sleeping and doused our clothing with every insect powder imaginable, but they multiplied apace. Behind the lines we build delousing rooms we called *Lousoleums*.

The pernicious insects were unconquerable, though picking them off was not the only means of dealing with these vermin. In two anecdotes Artur and his colleagues find out that ants and sweat are their "allies in the fight against lice," which seemed to be the only way to deal with the infestation.

In terms of disease, the unhealthy conditions led to trench foot, not to mention diseases such as measles and influenza, which caused casualties beyond those actually wounded in battle. Military censors were reluctant to discuss the spread of influenza among the troops, but Paul Ewald notes that the close quarters were ideal breeding grounds for the disease that was to kill millions of people during 1917–1918.[28] Artur makes no reference to this deadly viral infection, and it is likely that he was one of the fortunate ones who were stationed in an epidemic-free area. On the other hand, he does mention measles after the fierce battle at the Bois de Caillette, for which the medics provide a panacea for the infected soldiers: "Each one received some opium drops. We were all so exhausted that we couldn't go more than fifty steps at a time before having to rest."

The medical care that Artur and his comrades are given is variable at best, often due to the immediacy of front line care in terrible conditions, and subsequently differing opinions at the hospitals behind the front on who should actually be retained for treatment and who was healthy enough to return to the fighting. The first time he is wounded, he is transported to a field hospital in a renovated school some distance behind the front after being initially taken care of by the field medics and ambulances. During the time he spent there he became acquainted with a man who seemed perfectly healthy. A bullet to the head had left him with a mental disability, mainly due to the fact that it had lodged near the brain. Though it is clear that this was inoperable and that it caused immediate physical impairment—indeed, doctors noted in a medical journal that this was a unique and noteworthy case—the fact that he was not indisposed led to him being deemed healthy enough to return to combat. Artur suggests that the reasons were that they did not wish to demobilize the soldier: "He was sent back to the front without reference to his condition. With this solution they had avoided a situation which could have caused great difficulty in explaining it in writing and perhaps could even have been a reason for giving him a pension." While the front line doctors considered this poor soldier unfit for duty, the garrison doctors did not concur, and he seems to have been bounced back and forth as the differing opinions came into play.

Artur's own care after being wounded by a cluster shell in the vicinity of Rózan is also telling. Evacuated by medics from the front, he waits for transportation by supply wagon to a village church, where the Bavarian medical corps were in charge. He then is made to march a number of miles to a bivouac and then the next morning is driven to another hospital in an ambulance. Because this is full, he is directed to march to Prasznic, where a truck picks them up and takes them to "a real hospital" for his first "real medical treatment." There, after cursory attention, he is taken to a train and after two days or so they arrive at Osterode, where after four days he finally gets treatment for his wound by an actual doctor. After two weeks, he is among the fortunate ones who are not deemed fit for return to the front, and he travels another ten hours to Wernigerode in the Harz Mountains to recuperate. This circuitous route was not unusual for the wounded on both fronts, and moreover the pain, endless waiting, walking, jostling, lack of food or minimal food, varied forms of transportation, different doctors and medical personnel, and modest medical care until a main hospital was reached was considered the norm for German troops.

Throughout the memoir mention is made of the front line soldiers suffering from "shell shock," with effects that ranged from general lassitude to incapacitation. This effect, which today is considered to be synonymous with post-traumatic stress disorder (PTSD) took a toll on both sides throughout the war. While being wounded might supply some much-needed time away from the fighting, actual rest and recreation were in short supply and eagerly relished whenever they occurred.

Rest and Recreation

Official leave for rest and recreation was, as noted, different for the officers, who were allowed to return home several times a year, and for the troops, whose leaves were more sporadic. As Artur notes, this was often "meager" and by the last years of the war, all leaves were cancelled for the ordinary soldiers. As he notes: "I see that I really only had two rest and recreation passes between 1915 and 1918. These were between March 16 to 20 in 1916 and between September 9 and 18 in 1917."

Often times of recuperation went hand in hand with recovery, however, and in some instances this was coupled with actual leave. On the Eastern Front, Artur's company is assigned to construct roads using small birch trees, conduct regular night patrols and remove the bodies of dead Russians. On one night patrol he is wounded and sent to recuperate at a requisitioned hotel named Küster's Camp in Wernigerode. At this beautiful site, he is well cared for in good accommodations, with

Introduction

ample and good food, and has access to excursions into the Harz Mountains. He especially mentions the wandering to its highest point, Brocken. He is rested and relaxed enough to join a nurse, who is a pianist, and another soldier who sings, for impromptu concerts, performing on the violin in accompaniment. Indeed, these are later augmented by other performers on the guitar, harmonica, and lute in a civilized display of culture. He also has time to learn Gabelsberger stenography.

Artur returns to his company barracks in Stettin briefly before heading home to Berlin for leave. Indeed, this becomes a rare double leave, for this was the last time he would see his father, who dies a month later, and he is sent home again for the funeral. This is not precisely a rest and recreation leave, but the succession demonstrates that circumstances could offer time away from his military duties and could encompass both.

After these home leaves he is assigned to the border cities of Charleville and Tahure in Champagne. There the troops celebrate a meager, if restful, Christmas in France, his first on the Western Front. What ought to have been a festive occasion was only a momentary respite, which he describes as follows:

> The weather was mild with wind and rain. Our last work shift took place the night before, and on that day our tasks were restricted to only the most necessary guard duty. The day's post brought the much longed for greetings from home with small gift packages. We made it as festive as we could; the company was given an extra ration of food, wine, and cigarettes. The contents of the packages were shared with all in the company in order that everyone, even those who had not received mail, had a gift. But there were no evergreens in our vicinity, so we decorated beech and maple trees. Despite everything, the mood was quite celebratory.

Recreation in the trenches was sometimes accomplished through the playing of music, as can be seen in the photograph in Chapter 22. Here, Artur apparently was able to play his violin, demonstrating what these moments of relaxation were really like: "Common rooms were built, as were commissaries, and within the troop divisions that had musicians, concerts were held regularly." This picture shows that these rare instances could provide a modicum of civilized culture for the ordinary German soldier.

In terms of his rare rest and recreation leaves, almost all of these were spent behind the lines in occupied territory. Here, he notes the friendliness of the local population, all of whom extend considerable hospitality, perhaps even more than was expected or condoned by the officers. The usual commentary, "*c'est la guerre*," seemed to be a panacea against antagonism by the local population, and Artur is always grateful for these brief, rare respites.

It appears that his last leave was over a year prior to the end of the war, when, after the battle of the Meuse (which Artur calls the "Maas") the troops are marched to the nearest railway station for a ten-hour ride to the German border. They were anticipating yet another sojourn on the front, most believing it to be against American forces near Strasbourg. They were, however, taken to the Saarland town of Neunkirchen, where they were quartered among the German civilian population. While this may have been a de facto leave, the entire company was required to maintain military status with daily drills and practice, hardly the procedures for true rest and relaxation. Indeed, it is here that Artur reports an incident of incredible tragedy, wherein a couple of greenhorn recruits attempt to fish with dynamite and only succeed in blowing themselves up.

Although he does note that the ordinary troops were granted one home leave each year in principle, this was hardly followed in practice, and the reason may have been that the situation in Germany itself had deteriorated, both politically and economically, enough so that the command was worried about the effect upon the morale of the troops. On November 18, 1918, he and his company boards a train towards Strasbourg that would bring his service to an abrupt halt.

Aftermath

The collapse of the Reich in 1918 was one of the most difficult periods in German history. The Empire had only lasted since 1871 when it was cobbled together by the "Iron Chancellor" Otto von Bismarck in the aftermath of the Franco-Prussian War. The unification had been a somewhat awkward endeavor, with the King of Prussia being given the title of Emperor, but with the various rulers of the former German Confederation retaining their noble rights and privileges. With the rapid development that took place prior to the First World War, this situation became more and more superfluous in the face of a burgeoning military

Introduction

industrial complex, and Kaiser Wilhelm found himself possessed of more and more autocratic authority, supported by his military commanders. Artur comments at the last about the rapid development of military technology during the war, even as the Empire's domestic situation became more and more untenable. Up to the last year on the Western Front—the Eastern Front collapsed in July of 1917 and on March 8, 1918, the new Bolshevik government of Vladimir Lenin signed the Treaty of Brest-Litovsk ending the war with Germany—the lines were more or less stable, though offensives on both sides moved the territory occupied back and forth freely in a limited manner, especially in the Meuse-Argonne region.

With the American entrance into the war, a new and apparently inexhaustible supply of men and materiel began to sway the war in favor of the Allies, and the dire economic situation in Germany made continuation all but impossible. Ann Linder points out that Werner Picht coined the phrase "a gigantic death factory" which was a reaction to the war of materiel, the *Materialschlacht*:

> More than any other experience of the First World War, the *Materielschlacht* marked the men who survived it. From the German side of No Man's Land, the *Materialschlacht* was about one thing—the astonishing quantity of materiel (weapons, ammunition, food, and even personnel) that the Allies had at their disposal. Germany fought on two fronts until December 1917, and with its ports blockaded by Britain, was limited to indigenous raw materials and what foodstuffs it could produce. For the German troops in the field, the war of materiel was about survival, specifically survival against three weapons: shells, machine guns, and hunger.[29]

This is indicated in the memoir by Artur's description of the copper and brass pipes being torn out of a brewery to be sent back to Germany, presumably for war materiel, and in one incident that disturbed him greatly, he was required to take down the bell of a church for the same purpose.

The troops in the field were rarely informed of the true situation of the war, although it was probably clear enough that all was not well. This was particularly evident in the raw recruits that arrived at the front during the final months of the war. The rations that accompanied this "relief" was either scarce or "less edible," and "the uniforms did not display any longer the quality that we were used to," as Artur notes. Further, rumors of unrest in Germany came from those few allowed back on leave, and one cannot help but note that his constant descriptions of the relentless battles and lack of food underlie the desperate situation back at home.

This resulted in a virtual collapse of the German empire. On September 28, 1918, there was a petition for an armistice to forestall the revolution, but this was already underway in Kiel, and it soon spread to other regions of the country. On November 9 the Imperial government in Berlin was overthrown, replaced by a chaotic provisional leadership that lasted until the Weimar Republic was established in August of 1919.

For Artur, these events unfolded only gradually. After a march to the nearest train station, he and his company were sent along on a ten-hour ride to the German border. After recuperation for two weeks in Neunkirchen, as noted above, they headed south by train towards Strasbourg on November 18. He remembers:

> After a day's journey our train suddenly slowed down at four o'clock in the afternoon. We saw that it was coming closer to another train on the next track, which was giving the signal to our engineer to stop. When both trains met, several soldiers got off of the train meeting us. These German soldiers had no rank markings, but rather only had red armbands on their left arms. Likewise, their caps were encircled with a red cockade. An older man, who from the look of him and his bearing was an officer, asked after our officers. Of course, everyone in our train was wondering what the reason was for our stopping, and as many as were there got off. We gathered in the proximity of our coaches in which our officers were traveling and learned with anxiety that a revolution was going on in Germany. We learned that the German Kaiser had abdicated and that the people were being governed by people who had been elected.

At this point the troops become aware that their anticipated posting to the front near Strasbourg will not occur, and they are asked about their willingness to abandon the war and return home.

The officers were disarmed and placed under the command of a cadre of ordinary soldiers who were elected under revolutionary rules to be a governing committee. Artur notes with a mixture of sympathy and satisfaction that these oft-interrogated officers were now demoted to being just another citizen with no rank or privilege.

The train is then turned around for a trip back to their garrison in Stettin, though he leaves out what might happen from there. Indeed, as he nears Berlin, he is granted permission to leave the train to be with his family; it is not known when and where he was given specific permission to leave the German army, if he was at all. He comments on

Introduction

the chaos of this final journey, how the train system ceased to function in an ordinary manner, and how the revolution itself included a reverence for those who had sacrificed much during the war years:

> The moment the Kaiser left and fled the country, in many respects the situation was completely chaotic. This was also the case with the entire rail system. Our train had to stop from time to time because other trains had to be rerouted.... It was moving for us to recognize the happiness with which we were received.... Everywhere we were met with gifts in the form of fruit and food. We were all moved.

With this, Artur's journey as a soldier ends, not with jubilation or with tragedy, but rather with those mixed feelings that accompany the uncertainty of the future of a homeland for which he has fought for almost four years.

His Views on War and How They Changed

The entire memoir demonstrates a set of personal views that change drastically over the period regarding the reasons for the war. Early on, Artur seems filled with patriotism and enthusiasm at the German victories, including the Battle of Tannenburg. He notes: "We won, always won. Ah well, we knew this and more, but no one told us how many of our own were slaughtered in the pursuit of all these victories. It was only honorable and glorious to be a Prussian soldier," adding, "Think, what a great battle!" Perhaps this is just his immature patriotic belief in German propaganda, but it gives an indication of the pride he felt at the beginning of his tour of duty.

It takes but little time on the Eastern Front for Artur to realize that war is anything but glorious, and moreover that the reality is filled with horror: "The unpleasant, meaningless horror of war became sharply defined for me.... The depression that surrounded us was palpable. We only wanted to sleep. Exhausted and depressed we sank down to sleep off the evilness, only to awaken a few hours later to do more evil." The meeting with enemy soldiers under a brief flag of truce also reinforced the humanity of the enemy in a way that the propaganda of the military could not dispel.

When on the Western Front, he did his duty in often adverse circumstances, and while his views of the war, his commanders, and his situation became more and more cynical, he also was able to reflect philosophically on how the war affected even the natural landscape, which survived despite the ravages of battle:

> My first impression of this chain of mountains was overwhelming. I simply could not understand that human beings would make such a place of natural beauty a stage for war. And yet the deep valleys echoed with the bursting of shells. But despite four years of battle in the same area none of the evil of mankind could destroy nature and the magnificent beauty that the mountains offered in their majesty.

Here in the Argonne, the landscape itself shows his own changing attitude towards the war, with nature triumphing over the depredations of such a destructive war. Throughout the memoir, war is often compared with evil, while there is always a poignant description of nature, as if to say that this will survive, while the war will not.

At the conclusion of the memoir, he sums up the anti-war sentiments and relief at the end of the war in a simple sentence: "With jubilation we took advantage of this instance to be able to be finished with that insane life we had been forced to lead." He even graphically underscores it with what he describes as the cover page of an issue of *Simplicissimus*, a political, satirical magazine published weekly since 1896.[30]

Conclusion

Ann Linder paints the image of the Berlin to which Artur returned at the end of the war:

> After the Armistice, the conviction of having held the line to the end outside the frontiers of the Reich and of having marched home in order only widened the existing abyss between civilians and front line soldiers, who despite their sacrifices, came home to unimaginable chaos and misery—who came home, in fact, to a nation in collapse and revolution.... The full shock of being a defeated nation [finally] broke upon Germany with the revelation of the punitive and humiliating terms of the Treaty of Versailles.[31]

This summation, however, doesn't seem to be in concord with how Artur describes the soldiers being treated when returning home, as he notes an enthusiastic reception on the journey to his home. Obviously, Artur, like most of the front generation, wanted the war to be over after serving for almost four years on two fronts and being wounded in action. In his preface to the memoirs, he comes full circle and tries to

Introduction

grapple with the consequences of war. He found there as well initially no resolution amid the continued fighting of the November revolutions and the on-going deprivations caused by the war:

> I had believed that everyone longed for peace, but on the streets people shot each other. A revolution had begun and was in full cry. My longing for civilian life was great, but when I saw the poverty that gripped the German people, I had to ask myself if this was truly something to long for.

It was this conclusion that led him to immigrate to Sweden only two years later, believing that there, in a neutral country, at least he might find the peace and opportunity that eluded him in Germany after the war.

He was not wrong. As he notes in his preface: "I believed that the First World War would put an end to the grim horrors of mankind's history. But shortly thereafter countries began to rearm and 1939 saw a second war." A bare twenty years separated two conflagrations, each at the center of which was a German Reich. This time, however, it was to be a war in which technology reigned supreme, and while both Axis and Allies eschewed the use of gas on the battlefield, other weapons of mass destruction made up for the casualty count on both sides. Artur's statement—"The First World War marked the end of an epoch; it was the last 'human' war"—marked a dividing line between the grim personal contact between men and a way of slaughter that was more clinical. This change, along with the reminiscence of the horrors he experienced, led to his personal plea: "No War Ever Again."

Notes

1. Vejas Gabriel Liulevicius, *War Land on the Eastern Front: Culture, National Identity, and German Occupation in World War I*, Studies in the Social and Cultural History of Modern Warfare 9 (Cambridge: Cambridge University Press, 2000), 1.

2. Liulevicius, 14. This count is provided from military statistics of troops fighting in the East during 1914–1916.

3. Simon Forty, general ed., *World War I: A Visual Encyclopedia* (London: PRC, 2002), 120. Forty notes: "In the German Army the engineers were three distinct branches: the 'Ingenieur' Corps, the 'Festungsbau' (fortress construction) Corps, and the 'Pioneer' [Corps], concerned with field and assault engineering. The pioneers also assumed responsibility for many of the mortars, tunneling, and gas."

4. Martin Gilbert, *The Routledge Atlas of the First World War* (London: Routledge, 1994), 29.

5. Translator's note (Bertil H. van Boer): My grandfather's recognition of the arrival of the Americans contains a personal sense of irony, for among the early troops was my maternal grandfather, Captain Calvin Dudley Bush, who served along the same front as a supply officer.

6. For further information, see Frederick Luebke, *Bonds of Loyalty: German-Americans and World War I*, Minorities in American History (Dekalb: Northern Illinois University Press, 1974).

7. Christian Koller, "Enemy Images: Race and Gender Stereotypes in the Discussion on Colonial Troops. A Franco-German Comparison, 1914–1923," in *Home/Front: The Military, War and Gender in Twentieth-Century Germany*, eds. Karen Hagemann and Stefanie Schüler-Springorum (Oxford: Berg, 2002), 139.

8. Richard S. Fogarty, *Race and War in France: Colonial Subjects in the French Army, 1914–1918*, War/Society/Culture series edited by Michael Fellman (Baltimore, MD: Johns Hopkins University Press, 2008), 59.

9. Koller, "Enemy Images," 142.

10. See Note 3.

11. Alexander Watson, "Junior Officership in the German Army during the Great War, 1914–1918," *War in History* 14 (2007): 439.

12. See John Ellis, *Eye-Deep in Hell: Trench Warfare in World War I* (New York: Pantheon Books, 1976), 19.

13. Küsters' actual identity cannot be determined and indeed may be a pseudonym. In German, a *Küster* is a sexton or sacristan, an appropriate description of the function of this lieutenant as someone who oversees the details of the combat. The name is also a proper family name in Germany, so it is unknown whether Artur was concealing his identity or if he was actually identifying a specific person by name.

14. Watson, "Junior Officership in the German Army," 431.

15. In 1914, he had stated: "Undoubtedly this is the most stupid, senseless and unnecessary war of modern times. It is a war not wanted by Germany, I can assure you, but it was forced on us, and the fact that we were so effectually prepared to defend ourselves is now being used as an argument to convince the world that we desired conflict." First published in Karl Henry von Wiegand, *Current Misconceptions about the War* (New York: Fatherland Press, 1914). The original quote is in English.

16. Ann P. Linder, *Princes of the Trenches: Narrating the German Experience of the First World War* (Columbia, SC: Camden House, 1996), 53.

17. Bruce I. Gudmundsson, *On Artillery* (Westport, CT: Praeger, 1993), 36.

18. See *A Multimedia History of World War I* (www.firstworldwar.com, accessed June 9, 2011).

19. See Manfred von Richthofen, *The Red Fighter Pilot* (online text: War Times Journal, *Der Rote Kampfflieger*, 1917; translated into English by J. Ellis Barker, 1918). Online: www.richthofen.com, accessed June 2011.

20. Roger Chickering, *Imperial Germany and the Great War, 1914–1918*, New Approaches to European History 27 (Cambridge: Cambridge University Press, 1988), 95.

21. Al Mauroni, *Chemical and Biological Warfare: A Reference Handbook*, Contemporary World Issues, 2nd ed. (Santa Barbara, CA: ABC-CLIO, 2007), 66–67.

22. Translator's note: Although Artur Boer does not mention it, he himself survived a gas attack for which he was briefly incapacitated. For the remainder of his life, according to family history, he continued to have respiratory troubles due to this "wound."

23. The same month, the French and Italians completed the blockade of Austria's Adriatic ports, meaning that supplies could only be brought by blockade runners or overland from Germany's ally Turkey through the restive Balkans.

24. Linder, *Prices of the Trenches*, 62.

25. Ibid., 62–63.

26. According to Philip J. Haythornthwaite, *The World War One Sourcebook* (London: Arms and Armour Press, 1992), 381, daily rations were: bread, meat, vegetables, coffee/tea, sugar, salt, and cigarettes and at the officer's discretion liquor. The description in the memoir would indicate that this was a best case scenario, not the norm.

27. Jeffrey A. Lockwood, *Six-Legged Soldiers: Using Insects as Weapons of War* (Oxford: Oxford University Press, 2009), 80.

28. Paul Ewald, *Evolution of Infectious Disease* (New York: Oxford University Press, 1994), 110–111.

29. Linder, *Prices of the Trenches*, 61.

Introduction

30. It finally ceased publication in 1967. The actual issue of the magazine described by Artur doesn't correspond to those from the period 1916–1920, but the description may be a conflation of two issues: The first is from July 20, 1915, showing an industrialist hoisting a bag of money over a pile of bodies with the text: "*Die Hügel ist noch nicht hoch genug, Vittorio*" [The hill is not yet high enough, Vittorio], and issue 12 from June 17, 1917, showing a weeping death sitting on a pile of bodies under the rubric *Der Tod in Flandern* [Death in Flanders] with the text: "*Ihr Menschen, hört auf—ich kan nicht mehr*" [Ye men, cease— I cannot do any more]. Another alternative is that he may have substituted the name of *Simplicissimus*, a well-known magazine, for another less known one.

31. Linder, *Princes of the Trenches*, 152–153. Linder further explains the significance of the treaty: "Germany returned the territories of Alsace and Lorraine to France, along with the rights to the coal mines of the Saarland; territories in the east were lost through plebiscite and formation of the Polish Corridor. All her colonies were lost, the army was reduced to 100,000 men, the general staff abolished and any military air forces forbidden; the Rhineland was to be occupied for 15 years, and heavy reparations were levied based upon the infamous 'war guilt' clause, Article 231."

REFERENCES

The scholarship on the First World War is massive. Clearly this bibliography cannot encompass the totality of the vast amount of research that has been done on the four short years that comprise World War I. It is intended to show those resources which have direct application to this memoir.

Chickering, Robert. *Imperial Germany and the Great War, 1914–1918*. New Approaches to European History, vol 27. Cambridge: Cambridge University Press, 1988.
Churchill, Winston. *The World Crisis*. 4 vols. New York: Charles Scribner's Sons, 1923–29.
Citino, Robert M. *The German Way of War: From the Thirty Years' War to the Third Reich*. Lawrence: University Press of Kansas, 2005.
Demeter, Karl. *The German Officer-Corps in Society and State, 1650–1945*. Translated by Angus Malcolm. New York: Praeger, 1965.
Ellis, John. *Eye-Deep in Hell: Trench Warfare in World War I*. New York: Pantheon Books, 1976.
Ellis, John, and Michael Cox. *The World War I Databook: The Essential Facts and Figures for All the Combatants*. London: Aurum Press, 2001.
Ewald, Paul. *Evolution of Infectious Disease*. New York: Oxford University Press, 1994.
Fogarty, Richard S. *Race and War in France: Colonial Subjects in the French Army, 1914–1918*. War/Society/Culture series edited by Michael Fellman. Baltimore: Johns Hopkins University Press, 2008.
Forty, Simon, gen. ed. *World War I: A Visual Encyclopedia*. London: PRC, 2002.
Gilbert, Martin. *The First World War: A Complete History*. New York: Henry Holt, 1994.
_____. *The Routledge Atlas of the First World War*. London: Routledge, 2002.
Gudmundsson, Bruce I. *On Artillery*. Westport, CT: Praeger, 1993.
Hart, Peter. *The Somme: The Darkest Hour on the Western Front*. New York: Pegasus Books, 2008.
Haythorthwaite, Philip J., and Dennis E. Showalter. *The World War One Sourcebook*. London: Arms and Armour Press, 1993.
Higham, Robin, ed., with Dennis E. Showalter. *Researching World War I: A Handbook*. Westport, CT: Greenwood, 2003.
Horne, Alistair. *The Price of Glory: Verdun 1916*. New York: St. Martin's, 1963.
Jackson, Robert. *Fighter Pilots of World War I*. London: Arthur Barker, 1977.
Kitchen, Martin. *The German Officer Corps, 1890–1914*. Oxford: Clarendon Press, 1968.
Koller, Christian. "Enemy Images: Race and Gender Stereotypes in the Discussion on Colonial Troops. A Franco-German Comparison, 1914–1923." In *Home/Front: The Military,*

War and Gender in Twentieth-Century Germany edited by Karen Hagemann and Stefanie Schüler-Springorum, 139–157. Oxford: Berg, 2002.

Lengel, Edward G. *World War I Memories: An Annotated Bibliography of Personal Accounts Published in English Since 1919.* Lanham, MD: Scarecrow Press, 2004.

Linder, Ann P. *Princes of the Trenches: Narrating the German Experience of the First World War.* Columbia, SC: Camden House, 1996.

Liulevicius, Vejas Gabriel. *War Land on the Eastern Front: Culture, National Identity, and German Occupation in World War I.* Studies in the Social and Cultural History of Modern Warfare 9. Cambridge: Cambridge University Press, 2000.

Lockwood, Jeffrey A. *Six-legged Soldiers: Using Insects as Weapons of War.* New York: Oxford University Press, 2009.

Luebke, Frederick. *Bonds of Loyalty: German-Americans and World War*, Minorities in American History. Dekalb: Northern Illinois University Press, 1974.

Mauroni, Al. *Chemical and Biological Warfare: A Reference Handbook.* Contemporary World Issues. 2nd ed. Santa Barbara, CA: ABC-CLIO, 2007.

A Multimedia History of World War I. www.firstworldwar.com. Accessed June 9, 2011.

Neiberg, Michael S., ed. *The World War I Reader.* New York: New York University Press, 2007.

Pope, Stephen, and Elizabeth-Anne Wheal. *The Dictionary of the First World War.* New York: St. Martin's, 1995.

Reynolds, Francis Joseph, et al. *The Story of the Great War: German Attempts at Verdun Merchant Submarine, The Great Somme Drive, Summary of Two Year's War.* Volume X. New York: Collier, 1916.

Richthofen, Manfred von. *The Red Fighter Pilot.* Translated by J. Ellis Barker from "*Der rote Kampflieger*," *War Times Journal* (1918). From www.richthofen.com, accessed June 2011.

Showalter, Dennis E. *Tannenberg: Clash of Empires, 1914.* Washington, D.C.: Brassey's, 2004.

Tucker, Jonathan B. *War of Nerves: Chemical Warfare from World War I to Al-Qaeda.* New York: Pantheon Books, 2006.

Waldman, Eric. *The Spartacist Uprising of 1919 and the Crisis of the German Socialist Movement: A Study of the Relation of Political Theory and Party Practice.* Marquette German Studies, I. Milwaukee, WI: Marquette University Press, 1958.

Watson, Alexander. "Junior Officership in the German Army during the Great War, 1914–1918." *War in History* 14 (2007): 429- 453.

Wiegand, Karl Henry von. *Current Misconceptions about the War.* New York: Fatherland Press, 1915.

Author's Original Preface to the Memoir

When we were called to the front in 1915, none of us knew what war was. The orientation officers had fed us so much propaganda that we did not see any issue with war at that time, but then we discovered problems directly thereafter. Even our enemies discovered the senselessness of their dead. How many times did the request from both sides have to call for a ceasefire?

Little did we know that the hell that dogged us in 1915 would be over in another three years. When we deployed we understood that freedom would be the reality or the war. We believed this at the beginning, but seeing many destroyed cities and villages, we became skeptical.

The worst that we soldiers experienced during the war was the gassing in France. In the aftermath not many remained standing. Everyone who was exposed died from the effect of the gases. This was the most horrific part of the whole war.

Three times I believed that I would be finished with the war. The first time was when Emperor Franz Josef died, the second when Germany's fortunes turned, but the third time I was right, for the war ended for certain in 1918. When I returned to Berlin at the end of the war, I encountered yet another reason. I had believed that everyone longed for peace, but on the streets people shot each other. A revolution had begun and was in full cry. My longing for a civilian life was great, but when I saw the poverty that gripped the German people, I had to ask myself if this was truly something to long for. They had possibly even less to eat than the German soldiers. But there was a reverence for even the most demoralized of the soldiers returning home.

Author's Original Preface

I believed that the First World War would put an end to the grim horrors of mankind's history. But shortly thereafter countries began to rearm and 1939 saw a second war. The difference between the first war and this one was that the latter was a war fought with technology. Thus, the First World War marked the end of an epoch. It was the last "human" war.

Artur H. Boer
1965

Chapter 1

The Call to Arms: A Mother

With banners flying and music playing we marched to the train station in our garrison town in the year 1914–1915 following a strict military basic training. Citizens lined the streets and waved us a last farewell. A few members of the families of our comrades decided to follow us to the train.

At the station, a freight depot, we were completely isolated from the civilian population. A long train rolled in and we took our seats. Before the departure, which was to take place late in the evening, there was a long period of painful waiting. The people who had accompanied us stood faithfully by for hours awaiting the train's departure, two tracks separating us from them. We were divided into groups of eight men in each compartment. After we had organized our seating and baggage, we all gathered around the window or in the vestibules of the coaches. Among the young women in the crowd could be recognized one or another from our training period, one whose face we wished to capture at the last moment. Cries both friendly and encouraging arose, and small gifts of friendship in the form of flowers or souvenirs were thrown to us. Some addresses to one or another of the girls found their way to the intended recipient. We weren't depressed. Did we not read in the newspapers how the brave Germans had broken through the lines in Belgium and Luxemburg? Did we not know how they had encountered the French army and because of them sometimes found it necessary to burn down whole villages? Had we not already overrun the most modern fortresses like Liège, Namur, and Antwerp? Our instructors had reported to us pioneers daily about the honor and glory of victories in the land of the enemy. We won, always won. Ah well, we knew this and more, but no one told us how many of our own were slaughtered in the pursuit of all these victories. It was only honorable and glorious to be a Prussian soldier. The Germans were even now in Warsaw on the way towards St. Petersburg on the Eastern Front. In the west, we expected soon to take Paris.

As I think of this chauvinistic madness that possessed us, I am reminded of an episode during the mobilization in Germany. A young volunteer was rejected because his chest size was considered too small. Angrily he confronted the doctor. "There is still room for the bullet of the enemy," he bristled. He was then accepted and called a hero.

Soon it was time to go. A comrade beside me cried out, "Farewell, Mother! We'll see you soon!" I saw an old woman in a grey shawl. I saw one of the thousand brave men who did not cry even though their hearts were about to break from the pain. I remembered this sight especially during the first battle in Russia.

The train was set into motion. We rolled onward determinedly for a day and a half, although we stopped occasionally at some station to receive provisions. Enthusiastic crowds met us at each stop; they showered us with food, goods, tobacco, and cigarettes in abundance. There were also fat, well-intentioned rich people and their flunkies who weren't certain how well they wished us. We already felt celebrated as heroes and burned with anticipation to arrive at the front. We passed the fortresses—Allenstein, Thorn, and Danzig. It was night. An ordinance officer came with orders to douse all the lights and draw the curtains. The railway man locked all the doors of the carriage. There was talk of attack from the air and espionage. Think about it, such excitement! Now we weren't so very far from the border in East Prussia where not so long ago Hindenberg drowned thousands of Russians. Think, what a great battle! We would do no less if ever we arrived there. Towards morning our train stopped at a small station. It was still dark, but a feverish rush to unload occurred. Our field kitchen stood on a little street in the village, and we were fed at the same time we were issued a hundred bullets per man. After we had stopped and loaded our weapons, the march began. None of us knew where we were or where we were going. We marched out of the village, out into uncertainty. We passed through yet another village before the sun rose in the East. On and on it went. The country road was horribly rutted, and from a distance we

1. The Call to Arms

Artur Boer at the front in uniform in 1915 (van Boer family archives).

saw an occasional farm on the side. Each hour the march halted for a five-minute rest.

We had been walking for six hours and our bodies were bowed by the heavy packs, the new accouterments, and the solid boots. Indeed, no one could even say that we had rested well during the transportation by rail. About eleven o'clock in the morning we arrived at a small village with a Russian-sounding name. A strange sight met our eyes that made us forget how tired we were. A Russian border town, but what a town! Here we saw the first signs of war: streets strewn with stone but no houses at all, just chimneys. Everywhere we looked there was nothing but naked chimneys. The whole village had been burned; the houses were made of wood or clay, but the chimneys were of brick and therefore withstood the fire. It looked like a cemetery, for truly every single home was in ashes, and only the cold, black chimneys were left. Here we met other troops. A company of wagons was going the opposite direction and we had to move to the side of the road. It was an artillery company with cannons and ammunition wagons.

We arrived at an open place filled with company tents and Red Cross vans. We saw some of the lightly wounded, but they weren't despondent. In a close confidence they told us that we would not have a lot to do at the front, for a truce had been arranged and it seemed credible that a peace with the Russians was at hand. None of us realized at that point that another three and a half long and bloody years were ahead of us.

As a pioneer company we always had our main camp headquarters about eight kilometers back of our own lines. According to the organization, this was intended to be a perquisite that was shown us as one of the top companies. The object was to minimize our losses as much as possible during the stalemate at the front. But one of the inevitable inconveniences was that we had to traverse a roadless and trackless Russia. Each evening before twilight we had to undergo a two or three hours march to the front laden with tools, building supplies, ammunition, and barbed wire. If met with a withering Russian fire that landed immediately behind the front, we could hardly clear the stretch with caution and stealth in four hours. As soon as we arrived we were allowed a ten minute pause and then divided up into groups and sent into no-man's land to dig trenches or lay and repair the barbed wire fences. It was obvious that we came under fire from the enemy suddenly and without warning, for the two sides were no more than fifty meters from each other. So there was nothing to do but to duck as quickly as possible with one's head to the ground, or to dive into some shell crater. We soon became so trained at this that the moves were instinctive; thus our losses in these circumstantial attacks were thankfully minimal. But it was worse to work so close when the enemy used flares. For many minutes the field of battle was illuminated, and the machine guns of the enemy used the opportunity to pepper any object there. God be merciful to anyone who moved a muscle, for he could be certain of having twenty or thirty bullets fired at him, with some of them hitting home.

It was not enough that our work was tense and dangerous in no-man's land. We soon had quotas to fulfill; i.e., each group was required to complete a certain number of meters of barbed wire fence. This increased the risk of being wounded tremendously. I have always wanted to meet the person who could tie the so-called Spanish riders made of barbed wire in the dark without injuring himself! On those occasions when a night attack was expected, we were divided up among the infantry, posted to the frontline trenches and machine gun nests, each with his ten or twenty hand grenades, so that as soon as the enemy attacked our trenches, they could pop up and counterattack. In Russia, fortunately, such dire situations did not occur all that often. This too was fortunate, for on such occasions we were as great a risk of being shot by our own troops.

Chapter 2

1915: Meeting in No Man's Land

One pretty spring morning at six o'clock our company received orders to divide up under the command of non-commissioned officers and go out on day patrol to the front in order to evaluate the positions of the infantry and to make whatever repairs were necessary. First and foremost, however, we were to attempt to do a reconnaissance of no man's land and the defenses. In my group was a young engineer just eighteen years old. Although he was a good fellow, he was not very bright. When we had walked a good while, we took up positions in a birch forest, and a marvelous stillness hovered over this spring morning. Suddenly we heard our young comrade cry out; we stopped, and he declared that he had heard something mysterious. He stated that the Russians were calling to us. Our corporal, a Pole, rebuked him, but the boy did not budge. He asked if he could peer out over the lip of the trench a bit. We warned him against it, and almost at once we ourselves heard a whistling from the other side of no man's land. We took our binoculars and looked out over the breastworks, where we discovered a white cloth between the birches. Before he could be stopped, the lad raised himself above the trenches with a white handkerchief and waved back. We consulted with the infantry post about what we ought to do. Our instincts told us that we had nothing to fear just then, but it never hurt to be cautious, for what we were considering doing was against the rules. Each of us hid a hand grenade and soon stood in the woods in plain sight. Then we saw a long line of Russian soldiers who waved us closer. Step by step we approached each other. Not a shot was fired. It was like a Sunday promenade, but it was also a moment filled with

2. 1915

tension. When we had come to within twenty meters distance from each other, one of the Russian soldiers—we saw that it was a corporal—made a sign. The Russians each took their hand grenades out and laid them on the ground. One cried out to us in broken Polish to do likewise, which we did. I won't deny that we were mistrustful, and I knew that two or three of us had a few egg grenades in his pocket just in case. We approached a few more steps and suddenly a conversation was in progress. First we discussed the question of whether we couldn't stop fighting one another. But here there was no agreement. The Russians wanted us to shoot our Kaiser, and we wanted them to hang the Czar. (Today, I am convinced that the Russians were more insightful than we.) Then we asked each other about the access of each army to the necessities of life. The Russians had a lot of eggs, butter, and meat, but they were without vodka and tobacco. On the other hand, we were well endowed with liquor and tobacco, but weren't able to procure much butter or meat. Unfortunately, this meeting could not go on for an eternity, although we both agreed to meet at three o'clock in no man's land to exchange our respective goods. After the Russians assured us that we need not fear a surprise attack before we were back in our bunkers, we returned to the trenches. When we got there, we signaled them with some whistles, after which the battle was renewed with a few shots into the air. Right then and there we found proof that people are not the ones who decide on war or peace; some officer or another got wind of the thing and reported our meeting to his superiors. An hour later officers armed with carbines arrived and posted themselves beside the bunkers with instructions to shoot anyone who dared to leave the trenches for another meeting with the Russians. The day after a new regiment arrived to relieve us on this sector of the front.

Chapter 3

June 15, 1915: The First Attack

We are not adults until fate has tested us. Even though we were twenty years of age, we were still boys. We still regarded such a manly life in the military as an adventure, each and every one. It is only when the depredations of war have affected the human soul, when its horrors make us weak and dumb, when in the face of an incontrovertible evil we come to recognize a trembling feeling that creeps up our limbs, and we lack the possibility of giving our feelings expression through uncontrollable weeping, then and not before the true, serious man is awakened.

During the course of the evening the order for the preparation and march to the front came. Early the next morning we were to storm two villages that were occupied by the Russians; we were supposed to capture and hold the highway called Czerwena Gora (The Black Road). This position was to the north of Prasznic. We had to be there by nine o'clock in the morning, for after that the road was to be closed by artillery fire. We would be isolated for twenty-four hours and took with us our so-called iron rations, which were to be used only in the direst emergency. When we arrived at the trenches, they were swarming with soldiers who were to participate in the storming. The first field batteries began to fire at the Russian advanced posts. Artillery observers sat with their night binoculars and directed the fire of the 20 cm/s howitzers against the various machine gun nests. Now and again the Russians responded with a few light shells which went up and over our position.

It wasn't until two o'clock in the morning that our artillery began to fire in earnest. This turned out to be a true slice of hell which laid

3. June 15, 1915

in ruins whole villages and closed off the roads supplying the Russians. We were supposed to be prepared to go on the attack at four o'clock. For two hours we sat in the foxholes of the infantry and waited. This waiting period was the most tension-filled for us young soldiers. How would things go? We had no idea of the real, serious situation, and this was good. I would never have thought that they would make us go out in the bombardment if we had known what awaited us. A lot of brandy made sure that many young boys didn't know the true seriousness of the situation. (I myself discovered that the majority of the soldiers that fell during our attack were under the influence of the brandy.) The thundering fire reached its apex and then suddenly everything went quiet.

Our company was mixed in among the regular infantry and found ourselves close to the machine guns with our hand grenades. At the command to attack we were not to go out all at once, but rather in bunches (with several men from each group with enough space in between). We said good-bye to each other. Someone pounded me on the back, and comrade who pushed his way by me pressed my hand in a swift farewell. That same moment I remembered the little old woman in the grey shawl on our departure for the front. That was his mother.

We pushed forward. Only single rifle shots sought to impede us, but they went over our heads. But it was still dark out. Then we could take it easier. Someone close by me shrieked out loud, and simultaneously it seemed like there was an evil swarm of bees above us. There were four of us who found shelter in a shell crater and ducked still unharmed. A shell exploded above us sending a shower of lead bullets into the surrounding earth. Among us could be heard fresh cries. We could no longer stay there and went forward out of the Russians' withering fire.

Dawn came and a light rain began to fall as we arrived at the Russian barbed wire fences. Behind the fences stood about fifty Russians with their hands above their heads in the plain sight. It was thus that we recognized that they were people who wished to be taken prisoner. I looked around me and saw that there were only ten or so of us. One thought coursed through my brain: Why on earth didn't the Russians simply try and wipe out our tiny band? But we had to do something quickly. We clipped away the wire that kept us from the prisoners to let them through. A strange sight met us; large, strong boys who seemed giants in comparison approached us. They looked entirely exhausted as they doddered and stumbled their way towards us. And when they reached us, one of them showed pictures of a woman and a child, while another pointed to his wedding ring. Still another fell on his knees and grasped my hand, but when he tried to kiss it, I drew it back. This seemed rather mysterious to us, for we couldn't understand how such big men could behave like children. But soon I too would come to realize what these men had just been through. I was struck by a thought and said to my comrade: "Praise God, so many prisoners. Let's take as many as we can, because it will be better both for them and us." We quieted the wretches down and carefully poked our way back to our lines to where they could surrender.

Soon we came to the Russian trenches, but what a sight greeted us! They were shot to pieces, and only here and there a depression remained. We saw a bone, an arm or a half a corpse sticking out from the ground. Just in front of the protective barriers to the trenches lay masses of dead of all types. As far as we could see there was no one alive but us. A few shell bursts behind reminded us that we had to go forward. In a village to the right came an active machine gun fire. We turned in that direction, but just then some of our own troops under the command of an officer arrived; they included us in their number and pointed us in another direction. The piles of sand just ahead were our goal for the present, and then we could try and help our comrades at the village through a flanking movement.

We passed yet another Russian trench. Here too not a living soul could be found in the pits; only the dead, but in back of them we found a wounded Russian soldier. His leg had been sliced by a shell fragment. He was conscious and stared at us with wide-open eyes; the lips moved, but he was too weak to talk. Alongside him was a small mound of sugar left by his comrades when they had to abandon this location in a hurry. It seemed that he had recently been supplied with a necessary tourniquet. I consulted with my colleague: What could we do? "Nothing, we have to go forward," he said shrugging his shoulders. We raised a white strip of cloth to mark the location of the wounded man and had to be content with the hope that he would be found by some medic. We saw masses of dead and dismembered corpses all around us. There were ammunition belts and weapons strewn about, which showed the panic of the enemy's retreat. Suddenly we came into the field of fire of the

3. June 15, 1915

enemy's flank and had to seek cover. We weren't many, and we had no support on our left. Finally we came to the piles of sand and saw a position there with rifles pointing directly at us at the ready. A bit further on was a tree-lined country lane. We would have made it there if our numbers had been larger, but there were only thirty or forty of us, and to the right our comrades were still fighting hard for the village. It began to rain hard. The pile of sand only ten meters to the left of where I lay held around ten men, and then no one. About five hundred meters in front the Russians suddenly made their move as they concluded a position in the trees would offer more protection, which we also realized from our position lying down in the piles of sand. This meant we had to be on our guard. Suddenly a third comrade to the left of me flew into the air to a loud noise; he shuddered and then was still. A bullet had pierced a hand grenade on a belt on his pack. My comrade beside me was wounded superficially. The former remained just half a body; it continued to rain and a cold wind blew. We received orders to fire as rapidly as possible in order to deceive the enemy into thinking we were more than we were. I thought, if the Russians only made a little effort, we'd be their prisoners, as few as we are. But they were clearly a bit insecure, just like we were. I fired a few shots and set my sights on the trees lining the road. In the high grass right in front of me I discovered a dead Russian; the passing of each of my bullets lifted his long, blond hair and a scrap of his open shirt. I froze at the sight, and it disturbed me. I moved a bit to one side. How did the situation look to the other side? How many more deaths? There were perhaps many already seriously wounded who were lying in the line of fire without being able to receive aid. Thus we lay there and watched each other. The Russians were uncertain of the strength of the attacking force, and we were too weak to advance further. As we lay there came the thought: I wonder how the situation really is. What has happened and of what use is all this misery?

An orderly appeared among us and asked how our company was doing. I followed him, for we were to separate out from the infantry and proceed on to another task. We met a medic who was out and about looking after the wounded. At my question about how it went for my company, he looked at my stooped shoulders and said: "We helped some from your group, but one of them is lying over there against the wooden stockade—dead." An indescribable feeling came over me, forcing me to walk over there and see who of those that I knew it was. The stockade where he was supposed to lie was about two hundred meters from the place where we were. I went over and found my comrade, and I recognized him as if he were alive. It was the comrade who had pressed my hand in the trenches that very dawn. For the second time that day I saw the picture: a little old lady in a grey shawl—his mother—who had so bravely waved good-bye to her boy at the departing train. A bitter sorrow engulfed me; everything felt so heavy. Yes, the boy had not suffered. There was only a small hole in his forehead and a tiny rivulet of blood. A good death. But—the poor little mother!—I saw many other dead from our regiment. They were lying about there, cut down by the withering fire of the Russians. I expressed my regret by grumbling over their luck in being posted there. The unpleasant, meaningless horror of war became sharply defined for me. How many children, fathers, and others wavered in uncertainty this hour regarding the fate of their loved ones?

Our company gathered in woods in back of the front lines. There weren't so many of us, and we missed not a few of our dear comrades. We received food and brandy, but this had no effect on us younger soldiers on that occasion. The depression that surrounded us was palpable. We only wanted to sleep. Exhausted and depressed we sank down to sleep off the evilness, only to awaken a few hours later to do more evil. But this tempered us as men.

Following that successful or half-baked attack in June of 1915 at the villages of Jednorzec and Stegna in Russian territory, the truce was broken, so to speak. The Russians had shown themselves to be easily shaken and to have only small, individual companies; i.e., these were the so-called elite troops that were supposed to offer us a more determined resistance. The Germans had received a bloody nose. On June 24, 1915, it was decided to begin a new attack to the west of the two captured villages. We only awaited fresh replacements for those who had fallen or were wounded in the last battle. We went back to our old camps and spent the time resting in expectations of new support. This time consisted of a daily exercise, training, and the building of new roads, as it always does in the life of the German military. In constructing these roads one couldn't use the usual methods, for there was a lack of stone thereabouts. But the rich forests provided us with ample material, and upon the receipt of new orders we began a reprehensible

3. June 15, 1915

felling of trees. Since I was a city-dweller, I considered it a great sin to chop down these young, pretty birches. In this manner we built roads kilometers long, even though the work was essentially futile. As long as they were used by columns of marching soldiers, everything went well, but when the heavy ammunition wagons rolled over them, they soon became pounded into rubble and unusable. They were more a hindrance than a help to the wagons.

Eventually the rations became better, and we understood from this that talk of a new attack was serious. To provide troops with rations was a black chapter in military life. To supply the provisions for the company took a wagon drawn by four horses which had to travel an entire day to the nearest supply depot for everything that the company needed.

We also received indications that the Russians weren't inactive. Our patrols reported that they worked a lot underneath the ground, and we suspected that they intended to mine our positions; thus we listened with the help of microphones for the actual sounds we could spot within the earth. But in all reality I have to say that we couldn't localize the underground diggings of the enemy.

One Sunday afternoon we finally received an alarm signal from the infantry. The Russians had ceased their grubbing and were apparently ready to detonate something, or at least to go on the attack.

A platoon from our company cautiously made its way to the front, while the rest remained in readiness. Our comrades had not yet arrived when from the woods in the vicinity of the trenches the detonation of the explosives was heard and a massive volley of rifle and machine gun fire from the Russian lines began.

The projectiles buzzed like demented bees through the bushes, and our boys had to fall flat and seek cover. When the pressure had eased a bit, the march to the front lines continued, even though we still had two wounded; an orderly on a bicycle and the adjutant to the captain.

Upon arrival at the trenches an uneasy quiet had fallen and only a few single shots were loosened. The Russian attack had been thwarted. But if one went to the place where the explosion occurred, one could see that the enemy had miscalculated. The mine intended to breach our trenches had exploded five meters outside instead. Our machine guns had made mincemeat of the attackers. A dozen Russian machine gunners lay just in front of our barbed wire fence.

Now we had regular night patrols in our sector. The first night it was our task to remove all the dead Russians. But one night we were met with machine gun fire from just a few meters forward of our position. Cautiously we retired back to the trenches and tried to figure out where this close fire was coming from. It so happens that the Russians had dug out their old mine tunnel and set up two machine guns in a crater only five meters from us. The results of this maneuver were found out by the infantry pickets in the next few days. A type of Russian sharp-shooter lay in wait in the closer explosion crater and fired right through our defenses. During the day, every shot of his rifle hit someone, which meant that each shot was a dead man for us. This situation got on our nerves, and therefore we assembled some twenty odd hand grenades, and one afternoon just when twilight came three men from our company caused a terrible massacre within ten minutes in the Russian mine tunnel. The result was that the Russians had to give up on their clever cover.

Next came a difficult night patrol of no man's land. We had to find out what types of Russian troops were facing us. We found out, all right, but not from the night patrols. On June 24 at five o'clock in the morning we went on the attack without artillery preparation. But this attack was doomed from the very beginning. Straight ahead lay masses of Siberian elite troops, who poured on murderous fire making it virtually impossible for the small troop concentrations to retreat. There our troops were, irregularly spread out on an open field and finding it impossible to move either forward or back. A burning morning sun made the suffering of our wounded more unbearable. Our company was given the task of being sappers right up to the enemy's lines. I have to say that this was an insane undertaking, because it was brilliant daylight out and there was only a distance of eight hundred meters between us and the Russians.

We arranged ourselves in the trenches with each man in our group a meter apart; I was the third in line. The Russians already noticed our maneuvers and an intensive machine gun fire was laid upon us. It wasn't long until we had three wounded, myself among them. Fortunately, the wound wasn't serious, but a continual loss of blood and the great lassitude that accompanied it made it necessary that we were taken care of by the medics. Ambulance wagons already waiting in the woods behind us were ready to transport the wounded. We crawled there and

3. June 15, 1915

a medic sergeant spied us as he himself sat in a shell crater answering the call of nature. He tried to raise his trousers and run to us, but suddenly he sunk out of sight. Soon he reappeared and came to us half crawling. We sat together in an old foxhole and soon it was our turn to help our helper; he had been shot in the rump. Eventually we arrived at the field hospital, where our wounds were taken care of, and we rested for several weeks.

It was a folk school renovated for use as a field hospital some six miles back of the front; here there were also nurses. We were under good care. After we had rested sufficiently, we began to become interested in the misfortune of our comrades. For the most part, they weren't so badly wounded and could move about freely. Among these was a comrade who appeared to have neither bandage nor show other disabilities. He seemed to be completely well. Finally, after meeting him in the garden of the school I couldn't let it pass and asked him after some pleasantries the reason for his visit to the hospital. He smirked at me and said somewhat surprisingly: "I usually am a little crazy sometimes, and this is why I'm here." I looked at him doubtfully without daring to say anything in return. Then he told me that he had been shot in the head right after the beginning of the war. He was believed to be dead until a medic detected signs of life. He was sent to the medics and they discovered that the bullet had gone into the skull with little damage, but it was lodged between the brain and medulla oblongata and protected by the brainstem. The doctor's report on the seriousness of his condition was logged into the hospital journal, and with special care our comrade would be able to be transferred to a larger clinic. The doctors were extremely interested in the case and many of them had studied the position of the bullet by means of x-rays. But not one of the most adept doctors dared to perform an operation. Our comrade recovered in the meantime and felt no discomfort with his wound. Finally, he was sent back to a garrison along with the other healthy soldiers. At the German headquarters could be found the foremost doctors who made themselves of service to the army divisions and competed among themselves as to who could send back to the front the largest number of soldiers. Thus it was with our friend. He was sent back to a regiment on the front without reference to his condition. With this solution they had avoided a situation which could have caused great difficulty in explaining it in writing and perhaps could even have been a reason for giving him a pension. Our young comrade couldn't tolerate sudden, swift body movements. Two days after his arrival in a front battalion, he had an attack and fainted. The bullet in his head had rubbed against a nerve. But it was not easy to go home, even though the doctors at the front found him unfit for field service. The doctors of the garrison considered him fit. Moreover, there was some hope that perhaps a bullet would end the problem. For this reason, our comrade had been back to the front three times. I don't know what his eventual fate was.

One hot summer day in July of 1915 I returned to the front after my detour via the hospital. Our division had moved a bit to the south and our encampment was in a Polish village. Once again there was a shortage of rations. In reality there was hardly any food at all to be found near the front. The depot was so emptied of useable food that our supply officers had been able to find only dried fish and vegetables for weeks. A loaf of bread was divided between four men, one hundred grams per man per day. We therefore resorted to theft. We knew that the Polish farmers had concealed their potato crop in deep holes in their fields. We sneaked out at night and obtained the potatoes we needed. If we were surprised by the farmer, we wrote out a piece of paper that was in lieu of a requisition. He was required to present it to the local commander, one of our officers, and demand payment. The commander, however, usually became quite unhappy and drove the farmer out of the room with his riding crop. But finally it became too much for our officers, and our captain read an order from the division commander one Sunday forbidding the stealing of potatoes. After he had read it aloud, he said, "But comrades, there are a lot of potatoes in this region!" The encouragement in his words meant that continued theft of potatoes had approval from the local officers. The officers were well supplied with food and didn't look thin, but they didn't have to do the same manual labor as we did. If they thought the rations were beginning to get to them, they went hunting for birds, and the post commissioner took them jam and wine. This only concerned the officers of our little band. It was different with the infantry officers in a normal regiment on the front lines. There, in the forward trenches, there wasn't a lot of difference between the lowest man and officers. Whenever we met, when we went out at night, we were the same lump of clay. How many times did we not have occasion to share our cigarettes with them.

3. June 15, 1915

We did this gladly, for we knew that their orders were much respected by their men. As usual, we had to maintain the roads, and the three platoons of the company alternated daily between the front, roads, and rest at the camp. But the food was still awful and there wasn't much in the way of work progress, for we were too hungry. Moreover, we weren't too well enamored with the work either. Day and night the artillery and ammunition convoys rolled towards the front. We knew that things would heat up soon. The heavy artillery with 30.5cm howitzers were positioned at the front. This time it was going to be something special. We couldn't miss the passage of the artillery out in front of our camp a little northwest of Prasznic. The front was as quiet as ever, with only an occasional burst of one or another shell from time to time. The positions had been so solidified that one could pluck flowers in no man's land. Nonetheless, it was but the calm before the storm.

One day we received orders to bathe and shave. There was a march to the nearest source of water, two miles to the rear of our camp. This occasion was always welcomed, and our moods were immediately improved. We bathed and exercised in a beautiful birch grove while our clothes hung in a special room meant for disinfection. When we arrived home we heard a rumor that the company was to be moved long distance. We guessed that this could mean all the way to Turkey, where the Turks and Germans battled side by side. The day after came a re-equipment of the personnel. We became better equipped and were given an emergency issue of rations. Then we were to rest before a long march ahead of us.

On July 11 at seven o'clock in the morning we stood in full marching order on one of the side streets of the village, and an hour later we began to move south. Now we realized that this was merely a further move towards the Eastern Front and no journey to another front, as we believed. The day was warm and the road bad as usual. We had to often call a halt to let the artillery and ammunition convoys pass by us. The longer we went, the closer together were the convoys. At last, the supply convoy of our own division came upon us. When a line of mobile bridges passed by, we knew that all were marching towards a larger battle. We heard from the orders that we were to arrive at about 4 PM. The clock, however, was five and then half past, and we had walked four and a half miles on bad roads in extreme summer heat. Our supply convoy was ordered to advance ahead of us and find a bivouac or place to camp, but an hour later they came back with an unexpected message. The march was to continue another ten kilometers. We continued walking around a large outcropping, and after a march of six and a half miles we left the road and made a camp in the woods. No one was able to fetch the food that the field kitchen had ready for us. Most just lay down and slept. At six o'clock the next day we continued the march after receiving coffee and rations for the day. We walked in an easterly direction. The march this day was not as long, and after two miles we caught up to our infantry regiment. We were now at the front close to Prasznic. The Russians occupied the village of Szla near there. Our task on the following day was to storm the village. For the remainder of the day we rested in a nearby forest. After organizing a light assault pack, we took our place among the infantry at the front. The trenches had light artillery already in place. The idea was that we were to surprise the enemy the following morning with close quarter's fire and thereafter storm the village. But this proved to be harder than we had thought.

Morning came and the artillery went into action. Our fire was weak and hardly answered at all. When we arrived at the time for attack, we were met by an infernal spray of machine gun fire from the village. Luckily, we didn't have many of our people in the open and our losses weren't great. But now the opposition of the enemy was strengthened by heavy artillery and after a two hour bombardment we came to within fifty meters of the village limits. There we worked feverishly to dig in, and it was fortunate that the Russians didn't have their artillery in complete readiness; otherwise we pioneers would never have been able to create a field bunker and initiate telephone communications with our artillery. Thanks to that connection we were able to save many people, and before the Russians could set up their guns to work effectively, our howitzers laid down a heavy carpet of fire on the village of Szla. By the afternoon, the village was in our possession after some close in-fighting. The door-to-door fighting in Szla was of little intensity. It was thus relatively easy for our infantry to incapacitate or capture the Russians.

Quite a dramatic scene was played out between a Russian lieutenant and a German major, however. The major stormed forward with his men and saw an officer who ran towards the attackers from a bunker. The major called out to the Russian: "Give up, Comrade, opposition is futile!" The answer was "Never!" They both fired their pistols

3. June 15, 1915

at each other simultaneously. The German fell at once, but the Russian was mortally wounded too and succumbed in the early evening. We dug a common grave for both of them.

North of Szla the attack on a large forest caused us many casualties, because the Russians had their positions placed up in the trees. There was no other way out than to set the woods on fire. We took 300 prisoners. By the evening, we had taken the entire Russian positions about Szla, and the infantry began to pursue the retreating enemy troops. The reserves and ourselves were to rest in the woods. But we weren't able to make much use out of it. Two hours after we had erected our tents came the orders to move forward again. The enemy had made a stand at the Orzic River; in particular, two villages called Podossje and Plonjava were occupied. We marched half the night in double time. Upon our arrival we fortified the advance posts and dug a trench. The enemy bunkers came under fire from the light field artillery. Before we could use our trench, however, the entire Russian side was lit up by fire. The villages Podossje and Plonjava were both set afire by the Russians. We patrolled the villages and confirmed that the enemy had departed. Another series of flames at the Orzic River illuminated the road. It was a bridge that burned. Now that we knew we had a river between the battle lines we could take things easier and send an advance party with signal capability over the river to reconnoiter the land on the other side. The rest of the night the infantry was strengthened, and we began to build a new bridge over the river. We had already chopped down a number of trees and made a temporary structure over to the other side. There we found a new bridge hidden in the woods. The Russians had cached new material for a bridge, conscious that the old would be destroyed. But more than likely they had no idea that the enemy would be able to make use of the material. In this manner we were able to hurry the construction and by eight o'clock the next morning our infantry, ammunition, and artillery all crossed to the other side.

Even though the enemy did not offer us hardened opposition, we nonetheless lived through daily small stubborn skirmishes. For the most part, these were scattered machine gun emplacements that hindered the progress of the Germans and subsequently led to considerable casualties. It was that time of year when the crops were at their peak in the fields, and, protected by these, it was impossible to pinpoint their protectors. We understood better the reason for the steady opposition when we came to the fortified city of Rózan. We had many difficulties making progress here. With special caution we neared the large forests, where the enemy had placed sharpshooters high up in the trees. We could not advance without artillery. Then it became the Russian tactic to set fire to everything they left behind, so that nothing would be of use to us. Even the crops in the fields were destroyed in this fashion. But with this, the enemy always gave us the signal to march forward.

On July 17 we came close to an outcropping that was supposed to be one of the most heavily fortified positions in Russia. Considerable preparation had been undertaken on the German side in order to be able to take the fortification. This was the Kreuzberg, as it was called in the German reports.

Our advance party received a warm welcome even before they were able to take up their positions. A massing of troops was only conceivable within the protection of the woods. The enemy, who knew the terrain better than we, caused us heavy casualties with the aid of long-range batteries from the northeast and southeast fortresses of Pultusk and Ostrolenka. Infiltration of the fortified area was difficult, because we didn't dare to use the mapped-out roads, for these were under cannon fire the entire time. We dragged ourselves forward on the terrain any way we could. Of course, we became very tired.

At Kreuzberg a heavy artillery duel ensued, and the Germans battered the enemy's fortress with the 30.5cm coastal artillery. After a time we saw the first of the Russian air battles up in the sky. Their Russian airplanes were constructed with more armor compared with ours, and thus it was difficult to damage them from the ground. We were convinced that, if the Russians had had many of this sort of plane, our offensive would have been impossible to carry out. These planes flew easily and undisturbed at an altitude 500 meters above us, taking no notice of our anti-aircraft batteries, which weren't as effective as they would become later on in the war.

Because we expected a fierce battle we hastily built up our reserve positions. We were extremely cautious doing this, for it seemed that the enemy could observe all of our movements. It was anticipated that this would be one of our most difficult battles when the time for attacking was ripe. But the leadership of the army didn't take this operation for granted, and subsequently the artillery bombarded Kreuzberg incessantly day and night with their largest weapons. The infantry made a

3. June 15, 1915

few false attacks that were met in every case with a violent machine gun fire. There were of course casualties, but our losses were not so great. We equipped ourselves with a steel shield behind which we could creep forward handily. The main battle consisted of artillery duels, however.

One evening we once again observed flames rising from the right and left side of the Kreuzberg. The decision was made to explore this fearful apparition in front of us by a night patrol. In all silence and with caution we crept forward. The night was pitch black. To keep contact between all of us in the dark was of course difficult. We nonetheless knew that, if the Russians had been on watch, none of us would escape their fire. We crept softly forward, and were already about fifty meters from the foot of the hill when we discovered a rather wide depression in front of us. Uncertain what this could mean for we couldn't see more than five meters ahead in the dark, we decided that every tenth man would advance and, if no one was shot at, the others would follow after five minutes. Our confusion was great when we discovered that the entire twenty meter depression was filled with barbed wire barricades. But strangely enough, only about half of them were actually spanned with wire. Fearful that these might be electrified, we attached a ground into the earth and cast the free end over the wire. There were no sparks to indicate current, and we clipped the wire apart. On the other side we approached the mountain less cautiously. No sign of opposition was noticed, but on the heights we could detect the silhouettes of soldiers outlined against the dark blue night sky. We stood still until we heard German being spoken. We now realized that the patrol from the second division had gotten there first. The Russians had thus given up on this important fortress a long time ago.

Once up on the hill we investigated the fortress. There were well-protected bunkers with good defensive positions, not only for the infantry, but also the field artillery as well. Now we realized after taking the hill why the enemy had retreated. Our artillery had pounded this position horribly. There wasn't a single protected room that did not have dead and badly wounded, and the majority were obliterated beyond all recognition. There were direct hits from the heavy artillery about every ten meters. In one casement that had been hit by a shell lay three men about a table, but a fourth stood upright on his knees leaning towards the walls. My comrade went forward to see if the man wasn't just wounded. When he reached the other side, he waved to me with his hand: "Come and look," he said. The Russian was dead and his entire profile was turned towards us, but the other half of his head was sliced off by a piece of shrapnel; no butcher could have done it better. The scene frightened us, and we left to help with the wounded.

Chapter 4

The Battle for Rózan: July 18–24, 1915

We knew that the Russians had sustained heavy losses and were forced to abandon such an important fortress as Kreuzberg. But if it had been easy for the Germans up to this time, now it was a slow slog forward for the attacking troops the closer we came to the trenches about a thousand meters in front of the fortress. It was primarily flat land and the Russians had the opportunity to show all their strength, not only their field artillery but also the guns from the fortresses Rózan, Pultusk, and Ostrolenka.

It was known that the Russians employed people to string wire behind our lines, and many times we repeatedly caught one or another Russian soldier sneaking past in the vicinity of our camps and battery positions at night. I personally experienced quite a nasty situation during the battle for Rózan. Numerous times the infantry in their trenches were surprised at night by an occasional hand grenade that was thrown into them, even though the enemy lay too far away and there was no question of open trench warfare. In each case after such an attack, a veritable torrent of fire ensued and the morning after one could find a dead Russian inside our temporary wooden barricade.

We received orders to strengthen the advance posts. In the evening some of our group took up positions at the posts. Our corporal ordered that each one of us, armed with hand grenades, in turn to investigate the area closest to the enemy's position and disrupt them in the same manner they had done to us. Two comrades went out and came back after ten minutes. Now it was my turn. I jumped out of my foxhole, and when I had the barbed wire in back of me, I crawled forward. Every ten meters I stopped and listened intently for some sound. The ground was dense forest, and during my crawl I encountered some fallen trees that I had to detour around. In this manner I lost my direction and moved too far northwards towards another division. After about seventy meters I detected movement in front of me. I perceived that there were two or three people in the bushes. I took out a hand grenade and pulled the pin, after which I took up position behind a tree. After deciding which direction to cast the grenade, I armed it and after three seconds it flew into the bushes from which I heard the sounds. Because I expected the opposition to open fire, I cast myself on the ground behind a thick tree stump. First I heard a dull thud and then the sound of the grenade only about three meters in front of me. It took me a second to realize that I had cast my grenade against another tree that was impossible to see in the dark. I buried my head as much as I could in the earth and expected the worst. Then came a loud sound of my own grenade exploding, knocking me almost unconscious and cascading a lot of dirt and vegetation all over me. Of course, in the next second, all hell broke loose and a swarm of bullets sung above my head. Nonetheless, I was so close to the Russians, perhaps only fifteen or twenty meters, that I could see the flashes from their weapons. I lay still and uneasy for about fifteen minutes until they quieted down. Then I began to crawl hastily back to the left towards the direction from which I thought I had come. In the end, I despaired over the path and thought about stopping or rather lying there all night in the crater made by the grenade, for the Russians were shooting at close range and I heard them speaking behind me as well. I managed to reach our lines, however, and was happy to be in one piece, when all of a sudden I was shot at by our own soldiers. Fortunately, it was not machine gun fire, even though it was still heavy.

To attempt to make oneself audible was impossible, and the dark prevented any recognition. And I had no desire to remain in the vicinity of our own positions. Using every hole and rock, I slunk forward and at last jumped behind an earthen wall. I managed to wind up in the post of a junior officer. Of course I was very angry and began to berate my comrades for shooting at me, but silence descended when I realized that I had dropped in on a completely different regiment. They had no idea that there were patrols about. In skulking around with my hand grenades I had wandered about two hundred meters north of our division

4. The Battle for Rózan

into a completely different one. My comrades meanwhile had counted out the time for my return and came to the conclusion that I had expired close to the Russian lines. But the rest of the company did not have to go out any more that night.

During July 22–23 the attacking troops had difficult work getting close to fortified Rózan. The infantry met energetic resistance everywhere. The strength of the enemy that covered the town was not strong, but after we invested their outer posts we found masses of dead. The Russian pioneers had also laid out anti-personnel mines in every small niche in the earth. Defensive artillery fire now came only from the fortresses of Pultusk and Ostrolenka, though with increased strength. For the most part, they used shrapnel or cluster shells, and this was the reason that we took such heavy casualties. A few days later, moreover, I myself and four comrades would get to know these weapons better.

As with other places, the Russians had not completed their defensive positions around Rózan. This was the reason for the success of the attackers. The morale among the enemy was now broken asunder. Only one who has been in the field knows what this means. Several reconnaissance aircraft still directed the Russian fire, which also caused us some loss of mobility. Our troops had been on the offensive for ten days without break and were showing exhaustion. A Hessian attack division now arrived to reinforce us, and combined with them on July 23 we stormed the fortress outside of Rózan. The most curious thing about this was that this battle was relatively easy, despite the fact we sustained heavy casualties from small arms fire. As we later learned, the Russians had used their cavalry in their defense, and these could not bring to bear much opposition, although they spared a lot of people. The retreat was covered by elite troops. We didn't take many prisoners.

Now the road to the fortress was clear and we expected a number of surprises from the Russian side. The city of Rózan was built on a meadow and behind the city ran the Narew River. The fortress was equipped with strong walls replete with field artillery and howitzers. On the night of 24 July the infantry drew back to reserve positions, and we pioneers went to work on the position for light artillery. We worked the entire night intensively, rearranging the Russians' old positions into our own. We reckoned with an attack from the enemy on the following day and didn't wish to suffer for lack of means of defense.

At night we positioned our own advance posts during the work. But because these lacked a secure no man's land, a figure approached us. The figure answered our challenge with a weak, yet clearly German voice. When he got closer we saw a German corporal, wounded and exhausted. He had his right arm in a bloody bandage. We took care of him and gave him something to drink. Then we took him to a trench where he received warm coffee. After he had composed himself a bit he told us he had led a troop during the day that had come under grenade attack. His men were killed and his arm crushed. He remembered only that he was able by hook and crook to bind his arm by means of a bandage around his neck, and then he wandered about in a daze until he was cold, and by then it was night. When the medic poked him he did not cry out in pain once. We felt it necessary to ask him if it hurt, but like a paralyzed man, he only shook his head. The medic told him that he could not do much, for the entire forearm was crushed. The corporal answered, "I know, I'll have to have the arm off now." We talked over the case with the medic afterwards and how it could be possible that such a seriously wounded man would not bleed to death, but rather could take care of himself. His answer was that the man had become unconscious following the blow and the blood had dried in the heat of the sun, and that this in and of itself was a form of protection. But of course the wounded man could expect a much more painful treatment in the local provisional field hospital.

Little did I know at that time that the night would be my last on the Russian front, and that I too would be near death.

As we anticipated, at about four in the morning the Russians moved silently without artillery preparation from their trenches towards our position. A light morning mist lay over the field and we expected that the infantry would soon take over the positions that we had built. Suddenly we were surprised by several short bursts of machine gun fire that came from our posts on the right side. Simultaneously our field artillery loosened some shells towards Rózan and then there was movement on the entire line. Despite the fact that we were really too weak to go into battle, we placed beside us our rifles and grenades. Exhausted by the activities of several days of work our defenses were quite sporadic. We did not consider that we were under strength. But thanks to an artillery observer, the relief troops were given the alarm and shortly thereafter our battalion went into action and a murderous machine

4. The Battle for Rózan

gun fire felled the first line of attackers. The following lines retreated at once. But now it was in our best interests to take the offensive and begin the attack on Rózan seriously. The field artillery was ready, the reserves rested, and the unfortunate attack by the Russians were merely a spur to further action. A group of infantrymen and flame throwers came to help us. The storming of Rózan had begun.

The Russians knew that of course that the Germans had Rózan in their sights and did not stint on return artillery fire. The area surrounding the city came under mortar fire, but the reserve line received considerably more from their heavy artillery. Our company suddenly was ordered to draw back into the woods, despite the on-going attack. Here in this forest the artillery fire had surprised an ammunition convoy. Ammunition lay strewn about everywhere among dead men and horses. We were now to take over the transport of the ammunition to a battery that was shelling Rózan. We accomplished well an order that was not easy, given that mortar fire was cascading all around us. We thought that we might possibly cache the stuff in one of the trenches close by. But a new attack drove us forward again. We joined up with a company of trench soldiers who had just come to the front. We were giddy with tiredness, but because a grim fate can give way to pure luck, we learned that just when we left the woods the battery that we had just resupplied had received a direct hit. Now it was up to the reserves once again. On the right front ensued a furious combat. Right in front of us the defensive fire wavered significantly and thanks to this bit of good luck we were able to crawl over the barricades into the city. It was just six o'clock in the morning.

We immediately set about cleaning up and patrolling the streets. For the most part, the enemy had given up; we only met a few Russians who surrendered without opposition, apparently glad to become prisoners. The right front had a more difficult time of it and fought for a time street by street before the enemy retreated over the Narew River that flowed just behind the city.

As soon as the Russians understood that Rózan was occupied by the enemy, they began a systematic destructive rain of fire on the city. This was a rather ironic situation to come under fire while inside a city for the first time. We were rather more used to seeking shelter from the shells in open ground. Here we also found tumbled walls of buildings and stone flying about that were a danger to us.

The supply train that followed us had no pontoons to make it possible to pursue the fleeing Russians, but a sort of sandbag filled with hay could be used just as easily. A platoon of the company was ordered to get the troops over. Hastily we gathered together hay and straw wherever a good supply was found and began to stuff the sandbags. We were occupied with this work when suddenly much of the storage all around us began to burn. The Russians had fired incendiary shells in order not to leave anything of value behind. Now we really had to hurry to escape with our full bags. It was our intention to take care of the many wounded Russians that were found in various houses. But the fire took hold so rapidly that we didn't have time to investigate the buildings. Moreover, we ran the risk of being wounded by the exploding rifle ammunition that was burning in those buildings where the Russians had been housed. Our ears continually hummed with the sound of ricocheting projectiles. We hurried to leave the city and seek a depression in the vicinity, where we quickly freed ourselves from our packs and weapons.

About five hundred meters northwest of Rózan lay a small estate. When the Russians set the city afire, they also tried to burn down the estate as well. The shells traversed directly above us and a windmill. We assumed that the windmill gave the enemy an excellent shot at us and we decided to set fire to it. We should not have done this, for the Russians realized then that there were troops in the depression where we hid.

Our supplies had been erratic during the days of the attack; we had not received any fresh supplies for two days. We looked into a garden and found some apples and carrots. We then returned to our packs to grab a bit of bread, for we were hungry. At the same moment we heard a shot from the battery that zeroed in on the estate. Believing in the good faith that these were normal shells that usually whistled as they sped overhead towards the estate, we stayed calmly with our packs. Then it happened: I felt something hard strike my neck and at the same time heard shrieking all about me. The Russians had sent a cluster bomb instead of a normal shell this time. This detonated right above us as we sat with our packs.

I felt a hot pain and noticed how the blood ran over my chest and back, but I still had the strength to go over to my other comrades. At the same time a doctor who was in the vicinity also arrived, and the medics took us in hand.

4. The Battle for Rózan

There were five of us who were wounded by this cluster bomb. But while the doctor aided us, one of my comrades expired. He had received a ball in his shoulder and probably through his heart. I cannot describe how it feels to be wounded. It was so miraculous to have walked away from it still living. I had the feeling of an intense tiredness, and everything seemed to me to be all the same. The doctor shook his head as he examined my wound: "If you hadn't really had the luck of a peasant, you'd have to be buried too." The ball had entered in the middle of my neck and exited through the right side of my throat. It was only a question of a few millimeters or else an artery would have been severed.

Now our field cook arrived and offered me a warm meal: peas with pork. Even though I had a terrific ache in my head and neck, I succumbed to hunger and wolfed down the first hot meal I had had in an entire week and my last on the Russian Front. We were now to be transported to the hospital and receive rest for a time after that damnable pursuit of the Russians.

Chapter 5

Transport to the Hospital

As mentioned before, we wounded would now come under the care of the doctors. Myself, I would learn how it was to be among a number of seriously wounded and would experience how they transported someone who was hurt. It was July 24, 1915. We followed our mobile kitchen for the two hour long drive back to where our supplies were kept temporarily. Two wagons were made ready, and we either sat or lay on them as we continued along the road to the closest medical company.

It was a warm day and the roads were extremely bad. After an hour underway I asked the driver how long we had to go. He answered, "That depends solely on when and where the medical company is marching." That was a diplomatic answer that one could interpret in several ways. After two hours we arrived in a small village, and from the church tower a Red Cross flag was flying. When we had taken our leave of the comrades who had taken us to this place, we were received by the medics. It was a Bavarian medical corps that had taken up residence in the church on this occasion. The church was made over into a ward. There were beds made of straw and cotton bedding lying on the floor in the four naves. Everyone seemed to be in a great hurry, and we learned that the medics were awaiting orders to pack up and continue their work closer to the front. After a cup of hot coffee, we lay down dead tired and instantly fell into a deep sleep. We lay there for two hours before the medic came and awakened us. Those of us who could walk were to make ready to follow the medics on the march. The wounded who couldn't would ride. The medics lined us up and we set forth marching in tempo. The tiredness and pain sometimes became quite difficult, but the comrades who accompanied us were very diligent in making the hard march easier for us.

5. Transport to the Hospital

After seven miles we came to an open field where tents had been erected and straw obtained as bedding. Twilight had already fallen, and we were given warm soup from the medic unit's field kitchen. The next morning it was packed up, but brought back for those of us who were wounded. We were driven in hospital cars up to about noon. One of my comrades, who had been wounded at the same time as I and with whom I had previously been friendly, had received a nasty wound. The bullet that hit him passed through his jaw and crushed his teeth. When we finally arrived at a church that served as a gathering place I had to leave my comrade, for his face was so swollen that he couldn't be fed successfully. The church was, moreover, full up, and we continued on. It was a very hot day and the pain only became worse for us.

In the afternoon we came to a small town. This was entirely civilian and inhabited for the most part by Polish Jews. These set up their stands on the town square and sold fruit and sweets to the soldiers. We were let off here and told we would receive further orders from the local German commandant. We sought him out, but were told that there was no means of complying with the orders. Because we were hungry, we asked to have some food, but this wasn't to be found either, though a soldier did dole out to us a bag of dry bread. We weren't in the best of moods on this occasion, but we accepted the bread and bought for a pittance some fruit from the Jews. We didn't want to stay in this place waiting for travel provisions any longer, so we decided to proceed on foot to the next place. This was the town of Prasznic, which lay about seven kilometers away. We slogged down the road as quickly as we could. Thunderstorms were in the offing and after three kilometers we sought refuge in a grove of trees. Naturally we were on the lookout for anything coming along the road, and finally we were able to follow in an empty truck, pressed together underneath the canvas roof. The road was torn up by many shell craters, but our mood was upbeat despite everything. A soldier from Württemberg who had been badly wounded in the arm stood up among the cries of pain. He said, "Let's forget about this! We'll still come home to mother." And then we arrived in Prasznic.

The hospital was headquartered in an old barracks that had been shot to pieces. It was here that we were to receive food and the first real medical treatment. While we waited for food, which was not yet ready, a rumor spread that a narrow-gauge train, which had its station in the garden of the barracks, was to depart in a few minutes in the direction of the border. As hungry as we were, we took this opportunity to continue on, forgetting about the food. We embarked in the little train drawn by horses and were happy to escape as quickly as possible from everything that reminded us of the front. We occupied the open cars, partially covered against the rain by a piece to tent canvas. Because it didn't cover adequately, we took turns sitting underneath it, even though it didn't stop everyone from being thoroughly wet in the end. Six hours later, we finally arrived at a hospital in the dead of night. It too was a building requisitioned for the wounded and sick, but for the first time we saw nurses. It was a comforting feeling for us, wounded, tired and dirty warriors to be taken care of by the hands of women. We immediately received warm milk and thick, wonderful sandwiches, which we eagerly wolfed down. Then we learned that this very hospital was in the throes of moving closer to the front. As soon as we had eaten our sandwiches, the nurses were to have taken us in hand and subject us to the obligatory measurement of our temperatures. We were promised more food as soon as this was done. But the comrades, among whom I was one, who knew what this meant and sneaked away from the process and hid in an attic where there was straw for sleeping. It was raining hard and drops were coming through the roof. I had a high fever and slept badly despite my weariness, and it was equally bad for the rest of my comrades. In the morning we received coffee and a sandwich again, and continued on our journey with the horse-drawn railway. With the exception of a few short stops, we came to the German border in the early afternoon; there a real train awaited us. After such tremendous difficulties we finally boarded a train that had numerous coaches. But there were too many sick and wounded that had been gathered together here for transport, and thus there weren't seats for everyone. We made do with the floor and benches, exchanging seats every so often. This journey too was difficult, even though we were traveling through Germany. At every larger station we stopped to let off a portion of the troops. For the most part, the hospitals were already overfilled, and in this fashion we traveled sixteen hours until it was our turn to find help. It was in a school that had been requisitioned as a temporary hospital that I finally came under the care of a doctor after a journey of four days, but even so I thanked the fates for the great mercy I received.

Chapter 6

A Time of Convalescence

After all the wandering about wounded, no wonder we were a bit skeptical of finally arriving at a place where we could stay. We didn't feel at home in the converted schoolhouse in this city, Osterode, either. The doctor, a very nice old chap, was the only one in town. In virtually all of the hospitals in Germany the wounded were tended by civilian doctors. Now and again a military doctor came and inspected the facilities, but the main purpose of these inspections was to separate out the soldiers that were almost healthy and return them to the various garrisons. This depended entirely upon the willingness of the doctor to oppose the early release of patients. The treatment we received in that little schoolhouse was extraordinarily good, and the nurses did everything they could to make us comfortable. The local civilians came virtually every day with goodies and flowers.

I had been there for two weeks when news arrived that a new troop of wounded were expected. The doctor undertook an examination of us in order to prepare a possible place for the new patients. Uncertain thoughts confronted all of us. Were we now recovered or were we to stay longer? The doctor came, looked at our wounds, and divided us into two groups. It was now my turn, and after a short examination he said simply: "Transport." We had heard that word often enough and it gave me a rather unpleasant taste. I was assigned to the lesser of the two groups. The examination was finished, and the doctor made a few notes on some of the medical files. Afterwards a nurse came to us and said, "Yes, comrades, we are soon to be parted. Early tomorrow morning you are to be put on another ambulance train and taken to another hospital. New invalids are coming, and we must have a place for them here."

This was quite unpleasant news, and we weren't happy to leave our nice caregivers. The second group, on the other hand, had even more occasion to be sorry, for they were released and were to be immediately sent back to the front again.

The next morning we exchanged our hospital clothes for uniforms after an ample breakfast; these had been disinfected and washed. Then we were driven in cars to the train station, where a long ambulance train stood. It was already full of other convalescent soldiers awaiting transport to other hospitals. There was a special car for those who had to lie down, but those who could walk were placed in second class coaches. Once more it was a journey with pauses at every main station where a hospital was to be found. If I had thought the transportation was difficult beforehand, now I was forced into an even harder test of patience. Naturally, they did the best they could to care for us on board the train. The orderlies went throughout the cars asking how things were going and passing out liquids and tranquilizers. We received hot food at the stations everywhere, but although we sat comfortably, it was no rest for us.

Our journey had now gone on for ten hours. They off-loaded comrades everywhere to be taken to the local hospitals. The train had become smaller, as the empty cars were uncoupled. We found ourselves in the center of Germany when, in the middle of the night, we were informed to prepare ourselves to disembark. We got off at the little town of Wernigerode in the Harz Mountains. Cars awaited us and drove us through the city. After half an hour on twisting country roads in pitch black night we arrived at an impressive building. This was our goal, a hotel which had been requisitioned during wartime as a convalescent hospital. It was called "Küster's Camp." As noted, it was in the middle of the night, but everyone was awake, including the nurses who welcomed us. They were caring, wonderful people. After a brief examination and food, we were given warm, wonderful beds.

As pleasantly surprised as we were by these nice people, we were even more so the next morning. We awoke late in the day. A brilliant summer sun shone in our hotel room, and the view from the window presented the most beautiful scene of my life, one I cannot forget. Küster's Camp was on a hill and consisted of three large buildings. The

6. A Time of Convalescence

entire region encompassed valleys and high mountains, clothed in deep, dark woods. On a peak directly across from us we saw the Wernigerode castle. The hotel grounds included a carefully tended park with tennis courts. All of this seemed like a dream for us. There were only two men per room, and for we soldiers this comfort was almost unbelievable.

We as patients took our meals three times a day in the dining room of the main building. We were also cared for by the infirmary that was to be found in each of the buildings. We could walk in the park when we wished, or could go to our rooms and lie down at will, and a wonderful day room was open to us at all hours. All of the people we came into contact with were wonderfully friendly and helpful. How could we wish for anything more? Thus the days went by; we slept a lot, as if each day was the last Friday. But many days I still couldn't enjoy the heavenly environment. Something was missing for me, despite all of the high living, as I grew stronger. This was quite simply contact with others, as odd as this may sound.

During my daily contact with the nurses I met a comrade who was in the cavalry. There were only three of us in the infirmary, the last clients of the day. The nurse was named Elisabeth and was quite interested in music, and during the course of the conversation we came to that subject. It turned out that Derik, as he was called, was a good singer. "Yes," I said somewhat embarrassed, "I myself play violin badly."

"But this is wonderful," Sister Elisabeth exclaimed, "We have to have a concert this very evening."

The nurse then demonstrated good skill at playing the piano. A violin was obtained, and we began to practice the music that the nurse happened to have. Our rehearsals were held mostly in the dining room in the evening when it was empty of listeners. Despite this word spread among the patients that there was music at the hotel, and soon it was impossible not to have people at our rehearsals. Then Derik discovered that there weren't a few among the patients who could play an instrument, and beyond expectations there existed so much musical talent that soon a rather mixed orchestra was formed, with instruments such as guitar, harmonica, and lute. We played music for the enjoyment of all.

The autumn days in the Harz Mountains were incredibly beautiful, and we were invited on numerous excursions. The city of Wernigerode often made the means available to us, and we had the opportunity to get to know the beautiful region. The trip to Brocken, the well-known highest point in the Harz Mountains was also an experience. Because it was the season when the fruit had been harvested, the people of the town inundated us with produce. At other times we were invited to concerts and other pleasant events in town. On Sundays clubs would often come to the hotel to entertain the patients. On such occasions many of the soldiers would become friendly with the girls of the town, having a great time in the hotel's grounds with them. In Wernigerode I myself got to know a man who became a faithful pen pal long after the war. A German Baptist minister asked that a group of people blinded by the war come to Küster's Camp for recreation. One day my roommate and I were asked by the nurse to give some of the books to the hotel library for these blind patients. The minister worked to translate these into braille for the occasion, and I got to know Paul in this manner. He lost his sight in both eyes at the beginning of the war through a bullet in his head. For all appearances these blind patients were happy and content, thanks to their leader, the minister. He was a brilliant, very experienced man who, along with his three daughters, dedicated himself to working for their well-being. Paul was extremely musical and studied music. Several years later I attended one of his organ concerts in a church in Berlin; I remember that Max Reger was his favorite composer.

I had been in Wernigerode eight weeks. During this time I read a lot and learned stenography. There was a correspondence school that offered soldiers courses in the Gabelsberger system for free. I took this opportunity and derived much pleasure from it. The time for our convalescence passed and one day I was called to an examination by a military doctor. Sister Elisabeth sent the message to me and my roommate in our room, leaving a letter and the address of the mayor of Wernigerode. We were to leave the letter and return with an answer. We knew that the doctor would soon begin with the patients, and when I told the nurse of this, I noted a sly look in her eyes, while she stated, "It will be all right." We looked up the address of the mayor and came to a pleasant house. The maid asked us our errand and asked us to wait in the salon. We felt rather uncomfortable in this environment, and my roommate was about ready to throw something on the parquet floor. The mayor's wife came, greeted us in a very friendly manner, and we gave her the letter from Sister Elisabeth. While she read it, I noticed

6. A Time of Convalescence

once again a smile on the face of the mayor's wife. The maid came in with a large tray; we were invited for coffee, cakes, and soft drinks. A pleasant visit between us was soon in full swing, and we conversed readily while the lady managed to drag out the visit for an inordinate amount of time after we finished our refreshments. Finally she looked at the clock and called for the servant girl. We were now given a large basket with fruit as a farewell gift. Of course, we now ascertained the real reason behind all of this and had a good laugh. We returned to the nurse, who said, "You understand, comrades, that I want to help you stay a little longer with us; therefore I smuggled you away from the staff physician."

We thus had another week to enjoy this high lifestyle, but at the end we were once more in peril. This time, an ordinary doctor came. We were all gathered outside in the corridor and admitted one at a time to see the doctor. The door opened again and the doctor saw me. He said, "Nurse, I need to see this man now." With that Sister Elisabeth took my arm and said, "A moment, doctor, I have just given him an errand to run for me." A mumble that could be interpreted as "Oh really!" came from the doctor. The nurse said to me, "You should go immediately to the park and not return until the doctor has gone." In this fashion she was able to postpone the departure of myself and many of my comrades. But this could not go on forever, and the day came when we took our leave with all of the most heartfelt wishes for good luck for our future. We ourselves were reluctant to leave these wonderful people.

Chapter 7

Back to the Barracks

After release from the convalescent care each soldier was sent back to his respective barracks to which he belonged. I was sent back to mine in Stettin. I was assigned upon arrival to a company that consisted solely of people who had been released from the hospital. The duties were light manual labor, and the main emphasis was upon exercise. But we weren't there long. On day during a very cold autumn I was once more assigned to an active company. First, though, I asked for home leave, which I received. I could still enjoy the two weeks in the arms of my family in Berlin. But this was the last time I would see my father, for he was seriously ill. After my departure he was taken to the hospital, and a month later I received a telegram calling me home again for his funeral and burial. By that time I had received orders sending me to the front again.

After having been a soldier at the front for a longer span of time, life in the barracks was a real pain, for one has to admit that life at the front had a certain freedom despite the discomfort and danger. Duty at the barracks was hard and proceeded routinely on a schedule, with two days of practical exercises on the range and two days on the Oder River building temporary pontoon bridges. Up every morning at five o'clock, exercise until six-thirty, a march of five kilometers and exercise until twelve-thirty, an hour's rest, then inspection in the courtyard, more exercise, and training on the obstacle course. Between five and eight o'clock there was rifle practice and theoretical ordinance training in explosives, as well as other weapons. Saturdays were taken up with basic training and cleaning.

During one of the inspections in the barracks courtyard the leader of the battalion came. He called "Attention!" This leader, a first lieutenant,

7. Back to the Barracks

was standing about a hundred meters from the company but still observed movement in our ranks. He went directly to me and asked me if I hadn't understood the command. I thought, "You really are stupid," but I remained silent. He put the same question to my comrade next to me. He remained silent as well. "Both of you will do one hour on report," came his order. That evening, it was determined that the two of us, under the eye of a corporal, would work off our punishment while the rest of the company exercised. The corporal came to us and took us aside. "You are a bunch of old veterans, no?" We had to admit that was true. "Okay, we'll meet at three o'clock in the morning on the obstacle course."

The obstacle course consisted of various obstacles, such as puddles, fences, trenches, and various wooden walls up to four meters in height. First we did some marching movements, and then we hid behind the tallest of the high walls and told each other some of our war experiences. "Now it is time to reappear and show ourselves again," the Corporal said. This maneuver was done a time or two, and soon the hour punishment was completed.

To move like a robot lay at the core of the dissatisfaction in each soldier; these were movements that would be ridiculous in the field and, moreover, simply dangerous in front of the enemy. The result of this feeling of dissatisfaction was that we resolutely volunteered for duty at the front again.

Chapter 8

France on the Western Front

If one was destined for service at the front one was granted somewhat of a breathing space. The mobilization and most opportune time for transportation from Stettin was the reality behind this freedom. We were thus able to move about freely any hour of the day we wished within the city limits, although we didn't receive home leave this time. The reason for the latter was that the front was in desperate need of troops and transportation had to be ready to move out at any moment.

The journey to the front itself was the same as I had experienced before; occasional pauses at many stations without knowing when or where we were. No routing was known, not even by the railroad employees. Everything was made as secret as possible, and after one and a half days we passed over the border of France at the city of Charleville in Champagne.

As early as thirty kilometers behind the front could be heard a thunderous rumbling that never ceased. This was quite different from Russia. After we left the train and continued marching in columns we met open transports that went back and forth to the front. Hordes of soldiers were found everywhere, all belonging to the widely varied sorts of weapons. But what came most immediately to mind were the heavily rutted main roads. Not even in Russia were these roads so full of bottomless pits, and everything was covered in mud a foot deep. The most puzzling aspect was that human beings too wore this awful mud-colored covering on their clothing and heads. It was now the month of November and the rainy season had helped to create the horrible condition of the roads. But what about the color?

8. France on the Western Front

I was about to get to know it personally. This part of Champagne was called by all "*Champagne pédiculaire*" or "*Luschampagne*," a name which derived from the eastern barren part of the land, where nothing grew apart from the most common of onions. Even the few hillocks had only meager vegetation on them. The trees had only about three feet of soil for their roots, and many of them that I saw were keeled over after a storm. The main component of the earth was chalk, and we had to deal with it for the longest time.

Chapter 9

The Stalemate in Champagne

It was three hours before we arrived at our company headquarters in the vicinity of Tahure. It was a late November afternoon. The camp lay at the foot of a small rise, and the company had natural forts built into three terraces in the hillside. Our fort contained one group, and the soldiers who met us showed the same appearance as all of those we had seen since leaving the train. One might have believed that their principal employment was in a mill, so alike were they in appearance. After we were divided into the various groups we were able to rest until the next day. Here the war was truly stalemated, unlike the active war we knew from Russia. We were there primarily to do manual labor.

Because the war was stalemated, it that meant that the enemy had something of great value to protect. In this case, it was the city of Reims. All of the villages in the region existed only as names on a map, for their actual existence had ceased long ago. The roads that could be found here were all the same and equally dangerous. They were only passable at night or in the twilight. Both French and German observation balloons were up both day and night observing every movement around and in back of both fronts. They also spotted for the artillery. Before the day was finished, we who were to go to the trenches were supposed to have arrived at the protecting underground passageways. These were sometimes more than a hundred meters long and proceeded in zigzag form to the main trenches.

In the front trenches themselves there was a bunker every ten meters, dug into the earth until there was about four or five meters of covering above. Down there in the depths all of these rooms were con-

9. The Stalemate in Champagne

nected so that there was the possibility of saving the soldiers in case one of the rooms received a direct hit and was demolished. These connections were the most important task that we had to do. On the other hand, during the night hours we worked in no man's land to renew and expand the barbed wire to secure the positions.

We newcomers had to acquaint ourselves immediately with the customs of the French. In Russia we were able to move about the terrain easily without being targeted by significant artillery fire, but on the Western Front we had to exercise the utmost caution. The artillery of the enemy controlled all of the roads and was able to fire upon even the smallest groups. Our own artillery also often gave us cause for concern. If we found a path that we could occasionally traverse in calm, most assuredly the very next day one of our own batteries would be placed in the vicinity. And then of course the enemy pounded the place ceaselessly with ordinance.

Soon our first Christmas in France was upon us. Our sojourn in Champagne was spent in troop movements in the trenches. Food was incredibly sparse, and for we who had to work, it was especially difficult. Christmas Eve in France, which should have been a festive occasion, was celebrated only in thought. The weather was mild with wind and rain. Our last work shift took place the night before, and on that day our tasks were restricted to only the most necessary guard duty. The day's post brought the much longed for greetings from home with small gift packages. We made it as festive as we could; the company was given an extra ration of food, wine, and cigarettes. The contents of the packages were shared with all in the company in order that everyone, even those who had not received mail, had a gift. But there were no evergreens in our vicinity, so we decorated beech and maple trees. Despite everything, the mood was quite celebratory.

On Christmas Day my platoon received the order to move into the trenches. We were to help the infantry build bunkers. A short rain of fire from the enemy had demolished the bunkers in a large part of the line. It was a miserable job, because the recent rains had helped to distribute the contents of the sandbags, which for much of it was the only protection against enemy fire. We came back exhausted, and the next night it was the turn of another platoon.

In the middle of our camp on a rise surrounded by bushes a small cemetery for our fallen comrades could be found. During the evening, those of us who weren't on duty at the front made it as pleasant as possible. At this time we had among us a soldier who had been ill for a long time but had now just returned to duty. He drew guard duty at the camp during the evening. Before I retired for the night I went out for a bit and struck up a conversation with him. He was a young recruit, and during the course of our talk I noticed a certain unease about him. In the belief that perhaps the recent Christmas had awakened homesickness in him, I attempted to mitigate his concern. That same moment a long, drawn-out cry of an owl came from the tall grove, and he grabbed my arm terrified. I comforted him in order to spare him embarrassment. When it came again, this mournful sound, he said, "Listen, it's not only that. I am thinking more of my poor mother. I am her only child." I did not quite understand him and could not find any words of comfort, so I crept back to our bunker.

The next day he was to go with our platoon to the front. But, as he confided in me, he was afraid. I explained that this was only the normal stage fright that plagued us all at times, but he shook his head. "I can't explain it. The feeling is something else."

At the end of the march we were divided into groups to work and string wire. The latter consisted of communications specialists and two medics. They were to take a borer, which was the usual tool required in order to erect the telephone lines. We were used to it, for a soldier in the field has to be ready for whatever. *C'est la guerre*, it's the war.

At a considerable distance from each other, we passed two by two over hill and dale, occasionally seeking shelter from an artillery salvo. We stopped at an ammunition depot to pick up hand grenades and explosive shells, and eventually came to the tunnels which led to the front line trenches. Before we departed for various parts of the front we determined a meeting place for the march home later. The group I belonged to was to erect a mine thrower and strengthen a sapper position. Another group was to demolish a ruin that prevented machine gun fire, and three groups were ordered to dig a connection to the reserve bunker. The young pioneer found himself with those groups.

Late in the afternoon after completing our assignments we assembled for the march home. At a junction post further back we rested a bit and soon one of our groups appeared carrying a man on a stretcher. It was my friend, the young student sapper. He was hurried to the nearest evacuation post. He had been shot in the belly, and the same evening

9. The Stalemate in Champagne

we received the news from a field hospital that he had died. For a long time I was reminded of him every time I heard an owl.

Our area near Tahure was, so to speak, a junction point for those troops going on the Reims region. But the possibility of a night attack was small. Two kilometers behind our camp was a railroad tunnel that the French had demolished once upon a time. But there was about a hundred meters of the entrance left, which the artillery had used as a storage depot for grenades, shells, and signal rockets. One night we heard a mighty explosion coming from the tunnel. Simultaneously our telephone post rang with urgent requests for doctors and medics. It seems that an infantry company on their way to the front had sought refuge for the night in the entrance to the tunnel, unaware of the dangerous wares stored therein. A few soldiers made a fire to warm themselves, and during the night the fire had crept close to the dangerous ammunition. It was a catastrophe with many dead.

The front near Reims did not offer many troops more work than we had. For the most part, it was routine guard duty for the soldiers on the front line. We often had the opportunity to observe the French lines through the artillery spotting scopes, and we could clearly see the beautiful Reims cathedral some kilometers in back of the French lines. One day we noticed that the French had erected a battery in back of the cathedral. Of course, the German artillery then targeted this position with their pieces. There was an immediate protest through channels accusing the Germans of shooting at the cathedral. Despite German explanations, buoyed by air reconnaissance photos, the enemy retaliated by firing even upon our cemetery.

It was not always possible to give our dead comrades a normal funeral during field maneuvers, especially when troops were on the advance. If we were stationed for a time at a camp we always dedicated a place for the cemetery. These were plotted on the maps and the names of the fallen and paces they lay were always registered. But during heavy fighting and when the company was on the move we were forced with others often to bury our comrades with only a temporary coffin made of tent canvas.

Chapter 10
Aisne in Champagne

Our underground work at the front lines often encountered surprises of the most unusual sort. In the vicinity of Reims immediately south of town we were to tunnel our way under the enemy's positions. Work had been proceeding for about fourteen days when we stopped delving slowly and found that we were still twenty-five meters from the French but had already five or six meters of earth above us. At the entrance to the tunnel the covering was only one or two meters. There were four of us soldiers in each shift. We filled sacks full of dirt, which then had to be transported to the trenches in order to be emptied. Ten infantrymen helped us with this task.

It was a morning in May. A two-pronged attack near Aisne was in full swing, and the charges from both sides were coming at a furious pace. The result of this fighting was that neither we nor the French made any special gains. The terrain was flat and didn't offer any particular strategic advantage, but even our respective artilleries were engaged in a fierce duel. We who were underground had been working solidly for six hours when we felt a detonation and rise in air pressure that extinguished all our lights. The infantrymen behind us called out that we were all buried alive. The tunnel had collapsed about five meters from the entrance and now fourteen men were imprisoned. We then began to work intensively at the site of the blockage in order to get some air, for the burrow we were excavating was only a meter high and sixty centimeters wide. After half an hour we finally saw the light of day, but we emerged into a shell crater.

The French had hit our tunnel with a large shell, and we discussed among ourselves the best means of getting back to our trenches. It was useless to continue to tunnel beneath the ground, which meant that

10. Aisne in Champagne

we had to attempt to get to our lines from the shell hole via no man's land. We could not wait until nightfall, for there was neither food nor water down there, and we knew that the enemy would triple their fire with the onset of darkness. We took the risk, and then one by one intermittently without regular intervals we ran back to our trenches. Of course the enemy saw our running retreat and took the opportunity to shoot at whatever moved.

Some were scared out of their wits, but we all arrived back without harm. The French certainly now knew from where we had come and continued to bombard the place they suspected our tunnel to be with shells of large caliber.

Chapter 11

Dirt, Lice, and Clay

One speaks of confusion and battle at a front line, and there are still many people certainly who have read with astonishment about the wars and conflicts between nations and peoples, descriptions that are as realistic as all writers of history could paint them. One reads of attacks, battles, and wild scenes of war, and the reader may think that this is all rather exciting. But very few can actually depict how the troops at the front occupy themselves during the day in between the battles.

In most older tales of war one is of the opinion that the warriors are able to draw back to their camps after battle to relax and partake of a calm and lively camp life, or perhaps even return home for a span before coming back to the battlefield and new escapades. As heavy and loss-inducing that the battles in World War I were, it was equally difficult and dire for us in the camps between the battles, especially in France.

The troops who in most cases had their strength decimated withdrew back into their trenches. The trenches and their use were solely a product of the war, for even up to 1914 the use of underground bunkers, life underground for protection from shellfire, was practically unknown. The larger the caliber of the projectiles became, the deeper one dug. I know that there were troops who didn't leave their trenches in France for an entire six months. This is easy to explain, for during certain times reserves and relief troops were in short supply. This was especially true when furious battles raged in many places simultaneously.

Already in Russia we had discovered how hard it was sometimes to take care of one's body and keep it clean. But it was far worse in

11. Dirt, Lice, and Clay

France. In Russia we were lucky to be able to do the most necessary hygiene in peace and quiet behind the front. We could wash and care for our bodies. This was because of the minimal artillery capabilities of the Russians during the course of the fighting. The huge Russian forests offered us often natural protection, and there was always to be found some source of water with which to wash our clothes. And too, in Russia most of the place was wilderness in comparison to France.

On the Western Front we often had to go far behind the front lines, often many miles, in order to find a place to bathe. Of course, there were canals and water closer, but in most cases these were so close to the battle lines that the simplest act of drawing water cost human lives. That was the experience that we actually had. It should be pointed out that one also needed water for the food. Yes, this is true, but this was fetched with a pair of horses every other day from miles away.

One time on a march we arrived at a larger place behind the front lines where we had the opportunity to visit, among other things, a swimming hall. Just as we finished washing ourselves the order came to continue with the march. We were only able to look at the wonderful pool with so much water. The circumstance of not being able to wash regularly and not being able to change clothes caused us much discomfort. But the worst plague was the pests that assailed us. Down in the bunkers, where soldiers who didn't have guard or other duty slept, were always filled with half-naked men. By the light of the wax candles everyone knocked loose the lice from their undergarments. This was a daily procedure, as much as we today clean our fingernails. It was the only important task we had to do during our off duty hours. It was normal to pluck between thirty and forty of the buggers off our clothing each day. During this occupation we soon became real "louse philosophers," dividing the lice into different classes. We learned their customs, their methods of creeping onto the body. We reported our daily catches to each other in wild and humor-filled news briefs. We sorted them by color and size into English, French, and Russians. The last were those that were the most dangerous of them because their bites were the worst, though small. We gathered them from among the sleeping and doused our clothing with every insect powder imaginable, but they multiplied apace. Behind the lines we build delousing rooms we called *Lousoleums*. We warmed our clothes to high temperatures or we downed them. Truly, we were inexhaustible in our inventiveness to rid ourselves of the pests. One day we made a discovery that was of great use to us. We were laying about with some infantrymen on a sunny day behind the front lines in a wooded grove and as usual began to delouse. One of our compatriots in a fit of ill-temper flung his undershirt from him to get rid of a few. Shortly thereafter we noticed that the shirt was completely black with ants. We had a good laugh regarding the exchange of a shirt for ants. "It is of no consequence," he replied, "I've another shirt left." But after awhile the ants crept off, and when someone went and lifted the garment he saw that all of the ants had dragged away the lice. It was a happy solution to our louse problem, and from that day forward as often as we could spy out an anthill, these insects were our allies in the fight against the lice.

One time we were relieved by another division in our push for the offensive in France and were to follow them as reserves. When we came to a small stream, it was our first opportunity to wash ourselves and change our underwear. In order to protect ourselves from drawing fire from the front, we did not raise tents, but rather dug foxholes about thirty centimeters deep within which to lay. Despite our exhaustion we were unable to sleep for long due to the night chill. This forced us to put on our dirty clothes on top of our clean ones. This helped a bit, but soon our plagues had returned. We didn't notice the pests so much during the march, for they didn't like body sweat.

As mentioned earlier, there was no difference in the front line trenches between the officers and regular soldiers with regard to living standards. Even the officers were infested with lice. One time a lieutenant overheard two newly arrived pioneers speaking and wondering what these lice looked like. He went over to them, stuck his hand under his overcoat and said, "Boys, this is what they are." Between the thumb and forefinger he drew forth one of the small devils that we were all blessed with. Outdoor life, the situation, and body's natural defenses were probably what gave us the strength to protect us from and to fight off sickness from these creatures.

Another plague that we had to deal with were rats. They could be found in the encampments, bunkers, and trenches. We could never eradicate them wherever they lived. We set up traps, laid out poison, stomped them to death, shot them, but still they survived. This plague became so prevalent in certain areas of the front, especially where the loss of life was greatest, a type of rat dog was requisitioned. In the beginning these dogs made themselves quite useful, but over time they were increasingly rare thanks to the fact that the officers took them as pets or mascots. We had no means of protecting our food stuffs to any extent. The bread was often inedible. If we put the bread into sealed containers, the next morning there was a hole when we awakened. We made special boxes that we hung from the roof, but it was no use. The field kitchen had steel containers to protect our food, but apart from the grain and sacks of flour, we never solved the problem. The rats seldom went for the meat, for there was enough of that in no man's land among the fallen.

During the longer tours of duty on quiet fronts the soldiers sometimes occupied themselves with various handicrafts. We had heard that on the French side, the soldiers shot the most well-fed rats and made gloves of rat skin. I often felt a rat jump over my stomach during the night, but as long as no piece of bread was on my person that was nothing to be worried about.

Chapter 12

We Do Not Live by Bread Alone

    The lives of the troops on the uneasy Western Front were, contrary to all descriptions, not really so desperate as one might imagine. First and foremost there existed a comradery of the highest order, and if a sourpuss came among us who could possibly infect others, especially the young, we helped him to change his attitude. If it was not possible to bring a pessimist around to other thoughts, then we isolated him.

    Apart from fighting at the front and all of the work altering the terrain, there were of course periods of rest for us. After I studied my diary entries and the data in my old military passport, I see that I really only had two rest and recreation passes between 1915 and 1918. These were between March 16–20, 1916 and between September 9–18, 1917. What these leaves meant for us I won't go into closely. We set great store in being able to visit among the civilian population. The mood and reception among the French civilians could be quite changeable, but we always tried to maintain good relations with them. Those who were left in German occupied areas of France were mostly poor people who lived in reduced circumstances and in thrall to a foreign power. What we soldiers hated during our leaves was the return to exercises and barracks drills, which they tried to maintain even in the enemy's country. What we knew of life in the field and service at the front, our personal war experiences, were more worthwhile than all of the weapons practice and continual marching that we were sometimes plagued with during our leaves. On the other hand, we enjoyed the sports and baths. The leaders of the army had the opinion that we soldiers from the front had become sort of wild and that we didn't have the proper

12. We Do Not Live by Bread Alone

respect for our orders. Like us, those in command down the ranks knew better, but they were made to insure that orders were followed. Thus it could happen that, during the meager leave far behind the front we had to maintain the correct greetings to commanders. It was strictly forbidden during leave to go about speaking in a friendly, normal tone of voice to, for example, corporals and sergeants, as we were used to in the trenches.

At the front during the war a military newspaper with all sorts of news came out, which included the lives and customs of the troops, particular instances of bravery, and famous deeds. The comradery between higher officers and soldiers therein was mostly pure fiction. The paper was also illustrated, and thus there were pictures that proved this or another event. Of course, nothing ever contained a date or place of the event. The effect on us was that this paper had about the same veracity as the tale of the stork for a half-grown child. For example, about the time of the Battle for Verdun, a military newspaper reconstructed an event of how the German Crown Prince, who was a general in the army at Verdun, greeted the troops with enthusiasm in a village just behind the front. The picture showed an august man with his adjutant driving a car through a street. Behind the car ran about twenty soldiers. For us, the picture itself was for show, an advertisement; for we knew that the Crown Prince was generally known throughout the army as the "Butcher of Verdun." During the course of our movements along the Western Front we came into contact with various troop formations, and one day we made the acquaintance of a company of front line infantry. We spoke of this event as described in the military newspaper and were told that the real situation was somewhat different. Oh, the visit of the crown prince to the village was real enough, and he was received respectfully. The exhausted troops, who had just escaped by the skin of their teeth from the hellish front for a short while and were in great need of rest, were put to work cleaning up the streets of the village and practicing some sort of march for the reception parade. His Highness came, and the soldiers had to file past the crown prince and his retinue. As a reward they received an extra ration of meat and a mug of beer, and after a few hours the crown prince continued on in his car. His adjutant threw out a few packets of cigarettes from the car during the drive and of course the soldiers jumped to obtain them. A handy cameraman was there and took the moving scene as the soldiers (according to the newspaper) ran after the crown princes' car enthusiastically. No, the frontline soldiers weren't so crazy.

We worked alongside our officers and pioneers in many dangerous situations at the front, and a good comradery in the most literal meaning was of course the most natural thing in the world to us. Certainly we knew well who had the authority in the army or division, and who was given credit for the great victories; but we caught barely a glimpse of just a few of these powerful gentlemen. I know of only one time that a general, dressed as a commoner, was with us during a retreat. He was an old, white-haired gentleman who was with us during a fight, but he soon was recalled to the general headquarters by a courier. This occurred in Russia, which was little more than a maneuver compared with France.

When I think back to the war years, I have to touch upon at least once the thing that was so important for us soldiers, namely the question of food. To us, war offered the most variable unpleasant situations. In the beginning in 1914 the food was plentiful. Even the best was sometimes not good enough for the defenders of the fatherland, but at the time it was mostly the fault of the civilian population due to the goodness of their hearts. They didn't know how well or poorly they treated us. Only the hospitals could keep a certain standard. There, the food was good and nutritious throughout the entire war. At the front we either had feast or famine. This was dependent upon the various operations in which the troops were engaged. On offensives the soldiers looted the food stores of the civilian population in those areas where the latter had left their places. For example, one time we bought a large pig from some artillery soldiers for a handful of cigarettes. The same day the entire company ate fried chicken with rice and champagne. If we were on quiet fronts, the food was sparse, even meager. Sometimes we could obtain dried vegetables boiled in water with old pieces of beef which was washed down with fake substitute coffee. If the front was restless, we were cared for with the best provisions. We were given enough bread and oil, even fine jams. But on those occasions we only lived for the day. At the front we had the saying "Eat and drink, for tomorrow you are dead."

In July 1918 north of Reims in Champagne in France it was rather quiet. Apart from the usual repairs done in no man's land during the night, we kept to the bunkers and trenches, digging out new fox holes.

12. We Do Not Live by Bread Alone

More work was done during the day in the countryside that lay behind. As a result of the quiet on the front, our situation was extremely terrible. We had to share a kilogram of bread between three men each day with very little margarine or jam. Every third day we saw potatoes, and for the most part our warm food consisted as a rule of a mug of brown cabbage soup and a few carrots. The work and the daily marching took a hard toll on our strength. Each time we came to a work area we were allowed first to rest a half an hour before we began digging. As soon as the commanding officer was out of sight we cast aside our spades and picks, tired and exhausted. We were threatened in the beginning with various punishments, but when the officer saw that there was no possibility of forcing us to fulfill the prescribed work regimen, we were finally ignored. The leadership knew full well that the meager food was the reason for our lassitude and reported that even more admonishments didn't show results.

One day the entire company was ordered to rest and stay in camp. We liked this, but in the afternoon we were told to clean up for worship service. We were, to put it mildly, rather confused and asked: "In the middle of the week on a work day?" Well, it was to better morale, as odd as that sounds. After about a six kilometer march we came to an open field that was protected by woods all around. Many troops from our division arrived. In the middle of the field was a monument for enemy aviators in the form of a large cross. A mobile altar stood at the edge of the field. We were all wondering what would happen.

On many occasions when we buried our fallen comrades we had simple and eloquent devotionals. There were no ministers and our officers held forth with trembling voice a funeral service that no minister could approach. Why now would we have to walk such a long way just to hear a chaplain?

The chaplain arrived and began to speak. We weren't in a Sunday mood and listened to his words with indifference. But soon he began to spout a phrase that almost made us laugh: "We do not live by bread alone." We couldn't believe our ears, but it was true: they had attempted to console us with the help of a chaplain because there was no food to be had on that occasion!

There were times when we had to fetch our food from among wounded and dead comrades. This was the case with the advance to the Marne in the months of May and June 1918. As is well known, we

Religious convocation of the German troops, July 1918 (photograph by Artur H. Boer; van Boer family archives).

broke through at the Chemin des Dames, and from a strategic point of view for the Germans, it meant we advanced with almost every breath day and night. It was of course our intention not to give the enemy any breathing room or possibility to mount a defense. When we passed through villages or lesser places where the civilian population lived, we naturally acquired the necessities we needed. They always had food and drink. We couldn't count on our own field mess on these advances, for the supplies had great difficulty in keeping up with us. If we crossed wide territory we had to live on only bits of bread and what was in our canteens. We didn't dare touch the provisions of the enemy in their trenches for these defenses were more or less inundated by gas attacks. The food was therefore always poisoned and dangerous to one's health.

At this time our company was in the first day's attack on the enemy alongside the infantry on the front lines. We were relieved by other troops and thereafter followed in a slower tempo. In the hope of obtaining some hot food, our motorcycle brigade drove off to contact the field mess. They returned with the news that the mess wouldn't arrive

12. We Do Not Live by Bread Alone

before four in the afternoon. The clock was barely ten in the morning at that point. We hunkered down in several old English trenches to rest. As long as it was daylight we didn't dare to show ourselves outside them, for the enemy air corps was always on the lookout for such concentrations of troops in back of the front. We boiled some coffee and ate whatever we had left of the pieces of bread. Because we were momentarily disengaged from the battle, we could afford to rest and wait. But the day went by and no field mess came. We resigned ourselves to this at last and bunked down for the night. At five o'clock in the morning we were awakened by the watch. A mess orderly had come with a message that if we wanted any food we had to hurry up and come. The mess wagon lay on a country road and had been hit by a shell. Ten men took off with the cook to get food for us. They had to go a long way over difficult territory to get to the road while the enemy artillery did everything possible to prevent a movement on the ground. A horrible picture presented itself upon our arrival. The shell had landed between the mess wagon and the horses, which were shredded into hamburger. The orderly too was missing, apparently also exploded into small pieces. The cook sat wounded on the edge of the ditch and the mess wagon was tottering on only one wheel. The shrapnel had shredded the bottoms of the pots and the food was slowly dripping out of the mess wagon. Another orderly had positioned himself a bit behind the mess when the shell hit and so was able to save himself. Some of us took the wounded in hand while others attempted to save what could be saved of the food. Then the cook was handed over to the medics or other members of the company, and the mess wagon was tipped over into the ditch.

Chapter 13

Verdun—The Battle at the Bois de Caillette on Ascension Day, June 1, 1916

For three days we stayed with our division in a glen we called the *Kasemattenschlucht* between the forts of Vaux and Doumont. These were two of the many defenses outside of Verdun. The infernal artillery fire was omnipresent for everyone who was confined to this place. Confined together in small underground tunnels we were so tight that we all had cramps in our legs. Before any order for active movement we had to listen in total inactivity to hours of the shells hitting the earth above us. Now and again one of us would creep up to the mouth of the tunnel to breathe a whiff of fresh air. We lit candle stubs when we needed to eat. Because otherwise the candles took too much air we usually sat in the dark. To sit outside was rife with mortal danger. We became so apathetic that all topics of conversation were long exhausted.

Then a raging thirst reared its ugly head. There was a spring in the vicinity, but the French had cast the corpses of horses into it; we couldn't clean it because it was always under fire. During those times that the German artillery prepared for an attack with intensive concentrated fire, the enemy did not spare return fire either. All pathways were closed by their light artillery.

We still had to get water. Volunteers were called for and five men answered. Six hours later two returned without water. The others had fallen. In the hope that it would rain during the night we raised tent

13. Verdun

canvas to catch the drops, but the result was minimal. We chewed on the shoots of grass that grew here and there, but this didn't amount to much. The infernal artillery fire went on above with no slacking or abatement. Sometimes one heard the crash of 42cm shells.

Then the orders came: at four o'clock in the morning we were to storm the enemy position. At once the peculiar situation was about at an end. Then, at four new orders came: we were to postpone until six. The tension of waiting for that time took hold of us. Would the damnable pounding of the enemy lines be enough soon? Indeed, was there anyone left over there on the other side?

We borrowed a map from one of the officers, and on it we saw a path in no man's land that had to be passed. We had to pass through the opponent's lines through a rill to occupy a grove of trees, the Bois de Caillette. But at six o'clock orders came again to wait until nine in the morning. Now we wished to get out and obtain some sustenance. Our asking for food was not as important as our demand for water or something else drinkable. Provisions, consisting of preserved meat, bread, chocolate, and coffee, were doled out. We received only one mug of coffee per man, but if we wished it, then there was brandy in abundance. We swore against the orders that were able to obtain spirits for us, but not water. We saved the coffee in our canteens and took a slug of brandy. One always took advantage of the occasion.

We gathered together and were apportioned out to the infantry attack units. My group consisted of six men. We crept down to a shallow trench to await the order to attack. To while away the time and to allay our thoughts we had nothing better to do than play cards. Sitting in a circle, we remained there about an hour when our comrade furthest in began to moan. He declared he had been wounded. At first we didn't believe him, but when finally we began to show interest in him we found that he had a heavily bleeding wound in his belly. This must have happened when a little piece of shrapnel had penetrated our group and hit him. When he began to complain of a mighty thirst, we understood better and helped him to the medics.

We lost interest in continuing our card play and, after a long period of waiting in a rather unpleasant environment, we finally received the signal. But before we were to leave we wanted to know how our comrade was. We searched for the medic, who two hours earlier had taken the boy in hand. In the medics bunker we were shown a few men who were in the process of digging a grave. Our comrade had already died; he was the lucky one.

Now the attack began in earnest. The greatest difficulty for us soldiers was that in front line attack we seldom fought as a close unit of our own company. Here too we were blended in with other infantry. Before we parted we said our farewells to each other and made ourselves known to the infantry company we belonged to from this point forward. Equipped with hand grenades and a good supply of ammunition, we moved forward to the attack trenches. There the bunker soldiers were already installing flame throwers, with which it was thought the enemy positions underground could be smoked out. Now all we had to do was await the signal, given by means of a red rocket, to leap out of the trenches like a shot against the enemy.

Our advance was to take place after our artillery had cleared the way with its fire. The signal came and the charge began. Suddenly the opposition unleashed an intensive return fire against the attacking lines. The first stretch to the French trenches cannot be described. We charged forward more out of instinct than deliberation. We saw only yellow, red and white flashes around us. Through the steam and smoke one sometimes saw the figure of a comrade crumple and fall. The gap was immediately filled by others. We heard the screams of men blended with the infernal explosions of the shells. A stinking miasma of smoke threatened to suffocate us. But no machine gun fire, that which we most feared, met us. About every ten meters we fell into a shell hole to take a breather and to regroup. If our nerves were uneasy before the attack, now they were sharpened to the extreme. The air exhausted us and we cinched up our coats and tightened our scarves. Ever forward! To remain behind meant certain death. That was our only thought. The ground was riddled with shell holes. Dead bodies were being thrown up into the air. We trampled them. The terrible stench of burial places being uprooted assailed us. We were now approaching the enemy's trenches. A rocket signal gave the artillery a sign to redirect their fire. How did the French trenches look? Yes, we had to believe that they were fortified bunkers.

We lay in a four-meter wide depression. About us, half buried in the sand, lay masses of dead French soldiers. Here and there could be seen a piece of a human body. The mangled figures that almost appeared living. Clothing, uniforms, weapons, wagons and ammunition lay

13. Verdun

everywhere. A foul cloud of blue-yellowish smoke steamed over us, and now we received a new signal to advance again.

The goal was only a few meters off. We had to follow the direction of the shelling, advancing as if behind a curtain of fire. In the middle of the rill we nonetheless stopped once more. We had advanced too quickly and we were receiving flanking fire from the enemy's machine guns. These were installed to our left in the Vaux fort. Here we received evidence of French bravery. Despite the fact that our heavy artillery had hit this nest with 20.5cm shells, each direct hit found it manned yet again, four times in all. A few of our comrades in the foremost line who didn't understand the signal to halt fell before the enemy's fire only a few meters in front of us. When we were informed that our right wing had caught up to us so that we would avoid being in our own cross fire, we began the last stretch of the charge.

It lasted about three hours in all. We approached the Bois de Caillette, the grove of trees between the forts of Vaux and Duomont. This "grove" consisted only of burnt-out stumps, exposed roots, and a finely overturned earth. We achieved our goal and could relax and count which of our comrades were left. Our company began to storm this stretch of five hundred meters with eight hundred and twenty men. After a conscientious search throughout the 66th Infantry Regiment to which we were assigned, only thirty-seven were left after a three hour battle.

After our nerves calmed, reaction set in, and we collapsed all together. Thirst made itself horribly evident, and we thought of the water wagon that had to be somewhere close by. We saw it a bit to the left of us. One of the soldiers volunteered immediately to go after water. He was burdened with as many canteens as he could carry and took off after it.

The infantry formed patrols to investigate the area around us. We couldn't see the enemy, although we did care for a few wounded Frenchmen. A French aviator flew over us. This meant that we had to be absolutely still in order not to betray our new position. But it was not long afterwards that small bore shells began to whistle overhead. The opposition had still not correctly deduced our position, and we had to begin to build new defensive trenches immediately. The soldier who had gone for water returned and we drank ourselves to satisfaction for the first time in a long while. Immediately, several other soldiers went out after water, but they returned momentarily. A young infantryman handed back our canteens and with horror in his eyes only pointed to the place from which he had returned. The air was filled with shrapnel, and many corpses lay around the wagon. High overhead an aviator circled, leading the enemy fire to the wagon.

Within the Eighth Company of the 66th Regiment was a lieutenant by the name of Geyer. Throughout the entire battle he provided aid to his company by means of a whistle and white handkerchief. As we were working on the defensive positions he came to us, showing a very encouraging manner and speaking with everyone. Suddenly he said, "Comrades, it's still Ascension Day. Anyone who wants to be among the twelve can still apply." We thought this a particularly idiotic joke, since we had truly already lost enough of our comrades, and the situation was not at all appropriate for light chit-chat. We worked hard throughout the entire afternoon expecting either enemy opposition or strong artillery fire. During the time the order came to arrange a special protected place for the battalion commanders. We went to work with spades and pickaxes, building it of stone and great tree roots. All the while the enemy loosened shells between our new positions and our escape route. The great siege cannons spared the dale from their huge caliber shells, but lighter shells, so to speak, rained down upon us.

At twelve at night one of our platoon commanders, Lieutenant Küsters, arrived to lead us soldiers back. He stopped next to me and said, "How on earth are we going to get back through all that withering fire?" We turned around and noticed that there were shell craters in the earth all about, just like drops of rain on a flat surface. "Where are our boys? I can't find them." I made him aware that our "boys" had to be sought along that stretch. We then decided that everyone would gather at the craters and advance. But after an hour we could bring no more than nine men and two captured French soldiers, who begged us to take them behind our lines.

We all moved out. It was a singing and resounding hell. It was pitch black night, and the shells flashed across us. Shrapnel whined about our ears. There seemed to be only a slim chance in a thousand to get through with a whole skin. We jumped, ran, fell into every little depression in the ground so that we would not be observed. The only thought that consoled us was that we were not separated from each

13. Verdun

other. I still to this day do not understand how we twelve men somehow gained the protection of our own walls.

We collapsed exhausted when we reached safety. I looked at one of our prisoners and wondered if he perhaps did not have some water. He heard me and loudly cried, "*Oh, Monsieur, de l'eau, de l'eau*" as he held up his empty canteen. I immediately became ashamed at my idiotic demand; the poor sot had perhaps been thirsty even longer than I.

The rest of the night we lay huddled together out of exhaustion to overcome the worst stretch through sleep. We awoke somewhat calmer but even more thirsty. A medic company brought us water. We moved about in a dale among hundreds of standing, sitting, and lying wounded. We who could walk helped the more seriously wounded to the medics. But we were all in need of help, for measles had spread among the troops. Each one received some opium drops. We were all so exhausted that we couldn't go more than fifty steps at a time before having to rest. Now we only had to await the remainder of our company.

Our division was to be relieved at the front. It arrived during the course of the day, all sixteen that were left. This made a total of only twenty-six men out of 820. At last, when we gathered to march back to a more protected area, we learned that the bunker we had built during the night received a direct hit from a shell. Eight officers were killed, and among the dead was Lieutenant Geyer. Apparently he himself took the opportunity for the ascent to heaven.

Chapter 14

Comrade Karl Höhle
In Memoriam

He was our best friend in the group, our Karl, a very faithful and close comrade. His calm in all situations and his sense of duty to us was many times all that held the group together. Without rancor he often took upon himself the tasks of others and showed in intolerable circumstances what true friendship was. Born in Arolsen, he was the only one among us whose pleasant dialogue could captivate when he spoke of his home town. Love for home spread from him so that we all came close to homesickness.

Karl was with us during the battle at the Bois de Caillette, although we didn't see each other during the entire time. He wasn't with us when we retreated back to the division headquarters, and we believed that he was already to be found among the dead. In the afternoon at the main camp mail from home was passed out, among it a postcard for Karl, which I took.

Finally, very late, another few comrades returned from the front, and among these was Karl. These last boys were also extremely exhausted and, above all, thirsty. I approached the group. We greeted each other and were glad to have escaped the horror of the front. Karl asked for something to drink, and one of our corporals went to fetch his canteen. I turned around and had in mind getting Karl's mail in order to give it to him. Before I could turn back I heard a blast. The same moment that the corporal arrived with the water for the soldiers, a French shell hit a nearby tree and its splinters hit three men, with Karl most seriously with fragments all over his entire back. The doctor and medics were on the scene immediately and took care of the wounded. I saw that

14. Comrade Karl Höhle In Memoriam

Karl was conscious and thought that I would at least give him the postcard. A sharp word from the doctor saying that it was not the time or place prevented me from my doing so. But Karl nonetheless understood what it was all about and asked me to read the contents of the card. After I did that, he told me: "Write to my parents that I have been lightly wounded."

Karl and the other wounded were immediately transferred to the nearest field hospital, and at once I wrote exactly what Karl has asked. But we could anticipate the mail going out only on the morrow, and therefore I kept the message on me. The next morning we had just continued on the way to the army encampment even further back of the front when I heard in the company report that Karl Höhle had died before arriving at the hospital.

With his reply that he received only light wounds in my pocket, I didn't know what to do. I did not wish to be the first to report this sorrowful message. Not until four weeks later, when I assumed that his parents had received the message from the government, did I write a more expansive letter. The reply from Karl's home came immediately and his closest family asked me to tell them more about their dearest son. Karl was the only son in the family, but he had two sisters. I received many a care package from that family, which I divided with my comrades in the group. Later I received an invitation to Karl's home, as well. But unfortunately my home leave was always so short that I wasn't able to visit. And after the war I was too poor to be able to undertake such an expensive journey.

Chapter 15

The Ammunition Distributor in Champagne

Despite the inconveniences, the heavy burdens, and the danger our service at the front was so constantly changing and multifaceted that the interest in our work against the enemy made it easy to forget many difficulties for us pioneers. Patrol duty, mines and sapper work, the building of bunkers, bridges, roads and living quarters completely captured our attention. Our company consisted mainly of craftsmen and technicians in civilian life. Apart from this we had to have some knowledge of the ammunition required for various weapons and their purposes. We had to know the results of the various forms of explosives and the suitability of their use.

Our company had been posted to the front to the north of Champagne when a corporal and I were ordered to guard an ammunition depot. Besides the light ammunition for the infantry and artillery there were mines, hand grenades, and boxes of explosives for the engineering companies. Our job was quite pleasant, and the main task was to anticipate the daily distribution with the types of ammunition that the requisitions required. The distribution mostly occurred late in the evening or during the darkest hours of night. At that time the enemy had less of a possibility of observing the transport. The depot lay only three kilometers behind the front lines in a marshy wooded land. All of the ammunition was divided into forty huts that were fifty meters apart. Each hut contained about 500 kilos of ammunition, or about 20,000 kilos in all. All of this had to be available around the clock and tightly controlled, and yet our depot was one of the smaller ones. We had division and army depots which were well over ten times larger, both in

15. The Ammunition Distributor in Champagne

terms of size and contents. Each afternoon troops came to obtain ammunition, but the requisitions were mostly for hand grenades. These could be transported without difficulty, for they could be sent by freight wagons without the slightest risk. Blasting caps were worse, but the most experienced people took care of them.

My friend and I were sent twice each week to the company encampment to get our mail and supplies. One evening when I had arrived at the company I received orders that we were to be on guard duty, apparently for spies. The suspicion had arisen when a foreign soldier of an unknown platoon had posed some unusual questions to the sentry. When he was told to follow the guard to the commandant, he fled. The warning shot alerted the company, but despite a thorough search of the camp and the surrounding vegetation, we found no trace of the miscreant.

The reason for being especially cautious to prohibit foreign soldiers visiting our area was the placement of a division of elite troops here. Within a circular one-mile-area could be found our transport depots for engineers, radio, and telegraph companies. Then, in order to confuse the enemy, we built tank placements, but with these we undertook drills on an open field during broad daylight. The anticipated intention was that the enemy would discover this and alter their strategic plans, and thus we would be spared a second front line.

When we returned to our depot, we decided to keep extra watch on our area. For us, it was a disconcerting thought that our ammunition depot might one day draw the attention of some aviator. Moreover, we were enough to control the number of men who could obtain ammunition so that no one not belonging to the troop could infiltrate and blend in. But up to this point it hadn't disturbed our routine duties. As an extra task from time to time we had to try out old ammunition, which certain troops had returned, to see if it was good or not. For that reason we had nearby a logged out forest with old stumps.

One day during a trial explosion we sighted a French aviator. This was nothing unusual in and of itself. We ceased our work and camouflaged ourselves for the time being. The airplane circled at low altitude for awhile, then rose and let fall a few bombs on a useless road bridge. We heard the staccato of some flack batteries, but the plane escaped. When we investigated the area where the aviator had thrown his bombs we found one of them that had fallen into a marshy field. This was light and weighed only about five kilos. We did not understand the reason for the aviator's visit to us, but the events later on that evening provided us an answer.

About eight o'clock in the dusk a company of twelve men with two horse-drawn wagons appeared to obtain mines. The mines were of an intermediate size of about thirty kilos weight. Just as the mines were loaded we heard the growl of airplanes. This sound wasn't unusual during the evening either, for the enemy was often heard on their way to night raids behind the front. But this time they stopped above us and began to bomb the road that led to our depot. And these bombs were not the same light weight ones as those we recognized from earlier in the day. The teams of the wagons became nervous, and we advised them to postpone their departure. The horses were released and tied to some trees while we all sought shelter in a bunker in the depot.

In the belief that it was only coincidental that the aviators had released their bombs above us we made light of it. Soon even more airplanes arrived and began their bombardment. We were now seriously concerned that the aviators would zero in on our depot at any time, and we didn't want to find out what the conclusion to this would be, for including the team, there were not two but fourteen men in mortal danger. If one of the huts were to explode, then it was plausible that most of the rest would soon follow. A particular danger would be if those huts that contained our mines were to be hit, because they were on top of the ground and could be scattered over a large area by an explosion.

Among the team that made up the transport were two young fellows who had never been in such a situation of aerial attack before. They were not trained and had just newly arrived at the front, but their nervousness diminished when they saw that we who were used to such changeable situations were calmer. How the horses coped we learned only when the spectacle outside had ceased. We had been sheltered away for about half an hour when we experienced a very loud and deafening detonation. This seemed a long way off and immediately thereafter the airplanes went away. We crept out of the protective bunker and saw that the bombers had succeeded in setting the ammunition depot to the south of us on fire. This was the grandest fireworks that the enemy had yet incurred. The explosions, each stronger than the next, were an exciting theatrical play. Sky high fire fountains lit up the

15. The Ammunition Distributor in Champagne

heavens. We later learned that the bombed depot had just received three trains filled with ammunition from Germany. We heard detonations from that bombing for several days thereafter. Such a firestorm can never be quickly extinguished.

The suspicion that enemy spies had been involved could not be dismissed nonchalantly. The next day we received news that our camp would be moved closer to the front into underground depots. Large transportation columns took care of the move during the night, and after a week we were relieved.

Our somewhat easy life was over for this time. The entire division was once more set in motion. To where? And, yes, as usual, no one knew anything.

In calm encampments soldiers could sometimes cobble together some rather pleasant living quarters and environment around themselves. There were well-tended gardens, and the barracks were quite well-kempt and tidy. Common rooms were built, as were commissaries, and within the troop divisions that had musicians, concerts were held regularly. If one division left the camp, then the next took over caring for it.

Chapter 16

Outside Verdun Once Again

This was incontrovertibly the most restless corner of the Western Front during the months of January through April 1917. Following the storming of the Bois de Caillette, we came to recognize the intensity of the French defenses. From the point of view of the command we had been given the assurance that we weren't needed at the front lines, but rather our task was to build behind the front. But we didn't know that in this position behind the front lines we would be subject to the terrible withering fire that the enemy let loose upon the ground.

This began one calm afternoon when, equipped with weapons and tools, we went off to the supply depot where all of the material required for building defenses was stored. Dawn had not yet broken when the entire company was divided up into work and transportation groups. We then continued on our way towards the front. Nothing disturbed us on the road, apart from the sound of a violent artillery duel that could be heard to the left and directly ahead. We arrived at a camp of barracks that lay on a large hill. There we halted to rest. We had not stopped for very long before an infantryman came running and wondered who we were, and if we were aware of the area. Of course, he was told that we had no knowledge of the area at all and that we had just arrived in order to work on the defensive positions in this part of the front. Upon receiving this reply, he said, "Well, if you don't wish to be on the casualty list soon, you'd better scram and take cover immediately!"

He showed us the way to a deep trench which was already occupied by many soldiers. Still uncomprehending of the apparently dangerous

16. Outside Verdun Once Again

situation we found ourselves in, we followed his advice. The soldiers in the trench explained that the barracks we saw had long since been abandoned, for they lay in the most dangerous line of fire. Moreover, the only people we met were a single troop who were awaiting their replacements at the front and thus had been lying there a long time. They were used to the situation in this section of the front and, prior to continuing on their way to the front lines, they always rested in this trench that was built close into the mountainside. When it was dark, they moved out, as did everyone else who was aware of the customs of the enemy. This was, namely, that periodically they saturated the place with shelling, something we would soon find out for ourselves. In this trench could be found many large sheets of metal that we laid on the ground. As we heard how it was going at the front, suddenly someone cried out, "Heads up, boys, it's on the way." The next moment, after the soldiers dragged the sheets over the opening to the trenches, shells rained down on the glade in droves. The attack was not far off, but where we were nothing was happening. Pieces of shells whistled above us and hit the hillside, and masses of stone rolled over the sheets of metal. After awhile all was quiet again and the sheets were taken down. We continued on our way and came to a deep valley that was called *Höllenschlucht* or "Hell's Glen." This name had not been given without reason, as we were to find out over the course of the three months we were there.

Hell's Glen lay kitty-corner to the front lines and was the only accessible way to the front. At the bottom of this valley a narrow-gauge railway had been built to transport supplies to the front. Even though it was only the length of the valley, there seemed to be a large number of new sidings laid; why, we were soon to find out. This was our workplace and now we understood what transportation at the front lines really meant. The railway climbed towards the front, and our transportation column loaded ten wagons with much needed supplies and began to push them towards the high ground. After we had come a ways, it all broke loose. No less than a dozen shells hit the ground around us. We let go of the train on the tracks and hit the dirt. The wagons rolled back and hit each other, derailed, or turned over. It was a horrible mess. We returned, lifted the wagons onto the tracks and loaded them again. This time we wisely took with us a rod to stick behind the wheels if it became necessary to let go of the wagons again.

The narrow-gauge supply railway at the Höllenschlucht (Hell's Glen) near Verdun, 1916 (photograph by Artur H. Boer; van Boer family archives).

After proceeding a bit, we discovered that the track was broken by a shell impact. We pried up the broken piece of rail and replaced it with a new one, but before we had finished a new onslaught of shelling came. We sought cover on the spot. On the mountainside facing the valley could be found many places that had been carved out, and if one could reach one of them then there was no danger. But it was another thing to be able always to find a cave in the mountain or even be close to one, for it was pitch black night. There was a terrible confusion all around the wagons and we cautiously crept forward with them. When we finally reached the other end of the valley we had to unload them hastily and allow the wagons to roll back downhill by themselves. At that point we too came under fire again. This was not unexpected, for there was always a terrible noise and this echoed from the mountain path. Thus the enemy could easily hear us.

It was easy for the most part to protect oneself from the shells. But the enemy also used grapeshot in their shelling. I had already personally

16. Outside Verdun Once Again

experienced the effect of this and always felt a panicked horror. As a change, we now and again were given a bunch of shells to haul up the valley. It might be obvious that we were especially nervous about these. A hit in one of our wagons could cost the lives of a dozen men. I had seen this happen before at various times. Often after a direct hit on ammunition, one could find only a large hole in the ground, but one seldom knew how many men were involved.

Yes, we continued thus with our loading, running, seeking cover, and repairs. There was no other way to transport the material, and we could only count on luck to come through this work with our lives intact. Of course, we were all more or less injured by the slick ropes or broken rails which tore our hands and clothing.

Listening to the cannonade of our enemies consumed more of our focus during the work, much more than thinking about the wounds we received. Soon we were so well trained in hearing that we could tell which of the enemy's batteries were pointed at us. Yes, one might even remark that soldiers in the field can train a sixth sense through their hearing. In the way we escaped numerous dangers, at the very least.

Another transportation company worked about five hundred meters higher than ourselves. Up there was also a depot where the pioneers transported various sorts of materials for fortification work. The depot itself was already damaged, but the path that the company had to pass on its way to the front wound over a plateau. This plateau had many old trenches, which should have been used as pathways during the transport but were for the most part filled with the dead.

Now, we who had worked transporting things with our little railway were to exchange places with our comrades up on the hill. This job was by no means any degree of pleasant enterprise for us. The enemy had set up large searchlights at their front lines which illuminated all of the outlying high ground unequally. If any movement was noticeable, it drew a salvo of shells immediately. When we passed the high ground burdened with our long poles we couldn't enter the trenches at all. If we suddenly came into the illumination of the searchlight we had to quickly cast aside whatever we were carrying and throw ourselves to the ground. If someone shot at us, we took cover in some trench, and if this occurred, we made every effort to seem like the older corpses. A long time ago the high ground had been used for the long columns that brought food to the front. When the enemy had annihilated many of the wagons, the road was abandoned. But the dead still lay there. It was impossible to bury everyone who had fallen there, and thus they lay among the rotting food, and an unpleasant smell arose.

We had been engaged in this work for three weeks, when the remainder of our division was ordered to the front, and we were moved to a place closer to the front lines. This time we received help from the infantry for our transport work. Now, as we arrived at our closer work site, half of the company was once more given duties in the trenches with the infantry.

Our new camp lay up against the foothills and well protected from enemy fire. We soon made ourselves at home there; the food was much better and we had our own field kitchen in the camp. Of course, these were now good times in the camp nestled against the foothills. Down in the valley the French were very industrious in sweeping the place with their artillery. It was about this time that gas warfare also began, and many of us often made use of the gas masks that we always had with us. But we really didn't have any serious threat of being gassed.

The days passed in procession with no particular terror from the artillery of the enemy, and we divided our time between tension-filled marches to work, the work itself, eating, and resting. Of course, we lacked much while walking along the various roads and during work, and therefore we always had to carry along shovels. If we thought from time to time that we had it bad, we would soon experience something really awful. Yes, it would be a tragedy without equal.

In the middle of the foothill that lay directly across from us could be found a forest that had been completely destroyed by the enemy artillery fire, and the French still continued to lob their shells there. One dismal February day, a company of about twenty men loaded with materials came to that hill. They stopped at a place where we had often observed enemy shelling. They pounded spikes into the earth about a certain area and surrounded it with barbed wire. Later in the evening another company arrived with picks, shovels, and wheelbarrows. They were not armed but were accompanied by soldiers with weapons. Those of us who saw their arrival were confused by the nonchalant attitude they showed as they passed this most dangerous of areas. They began to work with their tools in the vicinity of the place that the first company had demarcated. We didn't believe our eyes as all of this took place within two hundred meters of our position, and so we grabbed

16. Outside Verdun Once Again

our binoculars for a closer look. The explanation became clear as orders when we discovered that they were captured French soldiers, who were supposed to do road maintenance within the field of fire. We knew enough about the international laws regarding conflict between two countries to understand that this must have been illegal. But we didn't entertain the thought that this was some form of retribution. Unfortunately, this was the bitter truth.

A couple of the German prisoners of the French had been lucky enough to escape and make their way back. These men related that the French military commanders used German prisoners of war to build fortifications within the operational sector of Verdun. They also reported that the feeding of the prisoners was terrible and insufficient. The living conditions were horrible beyond belief, and the result was serious illness and many deaths. The Germans immediately set about retaliating in the same fashion, and it was this that we were witnessing. At the same time, the enemy was informed of this state and told that it would continue unless the German prisoners of war were given better conditions during their internment. It was soon noticed that the enemy fire diminished in that section, for of course the situation for these Frenchmen who had to suffer for their government was well known. But until the entire affair could be resolved between the powers, the prisoners were kept in place. Night after night they were enclosed in the rough stockade that had been prepared. One has to consider that there was no roof over the men, and they had to spend many a night in cold weather without protection. They had it worse than cattle. Of course, the food was dismal, for they moved very slowly when they went to and from their place of work. We also noticed that they had with them drills each time they went out, and that their number seem to be decimated from day to day.

We witnessed this terrible play for about two weeks before it ceased. Apparently the conditions had also improved for the German prisoners of war. An improvement in conditions was also noticeable within our ranks from our officers for a time, and from this point on we observed a period of a more humanitarian stance in their orders to us. It was on the second occasion, as I shall relate later, that the orders couldn't always be fulfilled due to the so-called rigorous conditions. The purely humanitarian side of things was always observed for the well-being of our comrades.

I would like to discuss some of the prisoners that we often met and received. We noticed a remarkable difference in their view on being in such a situation. The Russians, as I have already mentioned, surrendered with fear, but the French demonstrated a certain proud and unshakable posture despite adverse circumstances. Among the English prisoners who came to us following especially difficult battles existed generally a feeling that the situation at the front was more or less some sort of sports game, despite the fact that human lives were at stake. Their demeanor was very nonchalant, something that was incomprehensible to us.

A certain difference between the enlisted men and officers among the troops taken prisoner was also observed. The officers were always correct and conscious of their responsibility. For example, a French lieutenant would give orders for the German officer of lower rank, who had charge of the transportation of the prisoners.

Speaking of such transportation, a unique experience needs to be mentioned at this point. During the offensive on the Marne during which the Germans took masses of prisoners, an entire French battalion surrendered. The attack infantry that were not needed at the front were mainly used as personnel required for the transportation. The commander for this movement was an old reservist captain. The French battalion commander was also an elderly bearded gentleman. First, they met each other with the correct military bearing. Thereafter, both officers traveled together side by side at the front of the column. It needs to be said that the German captain did not know French; likewise the French officer could not speak German. The march ahead for the column was quite long, and strangely enough, both officers shortly began to hold a discussion. This eventually became rather lively, and at last it erupted into a real dispute. The column arrived at the first stage of the march where the linguistically-capable soldiers had orders to sort out the prisoners for the continuation of the march. At this, the conversation took on a rather bizarre form. One of the German officers found out that both of the officers in charge were professionals with the same interests. In order to comprehend each other, they spoke in Latin. But during that strange discussion, they had chanced upon a common problem that had bedeviled them in their civilian occupations. Later when the war was over, they worked together quite frequently.

16. Outside Verdun Once Again

The subject of internment could also cause some reflections among us, and these were of the most varied types. But in the majority of cases, it meant that the war was over for a soldier who had been captured. Once we were engaged in building a bunker in Champagne, where the French had their patrols attack on a daily basis without advance warning. Because the position there was in a relatively quiet zone, the trenches were manned with less strength. There where we worked could be found only a few individual posts behind the breastworks. It was a magnificent afternoon, and no one could conceive that the enemy would undertake something. We were a single company and relieved each other in our work beneath the ground, so that there were always four below and four above at the entrance to the bunker. On this occasion we had our rifles a distance away in a trench. Suddenly we heard from the advance infantry post on our left a rather sharp machine gun burst. Since this was a daily event it didn't worry us unduly. But then the soldiers above us returned fire and an infantryman came running up to us exclaiming "The French are coming!" The four of us on top of the burrow looked out and saw that about thirty or forty men were charging at us. We called out to those below to hurry so that we could run over to the trenches and fetch our weapons in order to blunt the enemy attack. There were those fortunate enough with the help of the infantry to turn back the charge, but not until the French had penetrated our outermost lines. We then returned to our workplace, but we couldn't find our comrades there any longer. The French had taken them. A long time later we learned that their relatives had received a message from the boys in France, and that they didn't have to worry about them. These raids by both ourselves and the enemy served the best purpose of learning all about the opponent's troop positions and character.

Chapter 17

The Marne Offensive: Breakthrough at the Chemins des Dames

The continual movement of troops on the Western Front belonged to the orders of the day and the open transport of ammunition was a task that was not unusual for us. Of course, there was always some secret intelligence regarding some huge breakthrough that was being prepared by the Germans. There was talk that our division was to be the point of the offensive, or there was the rumor that the enemy was considering breaking through the lines. Truly, to react to such messages was difficult to do, for our circumstances were no different than those with which we began the war. We were more like an army of robots. The insane singular spirit of war that had led us over three years had completely killed off our optimism. The only thing left was our daily tension and the need for self-preservation.

At the beginning of 1918 we were hastily moved to a position that was unknown to us. We didn't expect anything special, for it was so commonplace during the last times it happened that we felt we lived like nomads without any firm army address. They called us therefore the flying division. The only thing that was unsettling was that our orders were in no way clear about our positions. Many nights we lay in tents in the woods, always alert. If occasionally we came close to a troop encampment, we found there was no room for us. Moreover, the orders to move usually came only a few hours beforehand. Without permanent quarters we arrived at last at several occupied trenches about five kilometers from the front.

17. The Marne Offensive

Immediately upon arrival came the orders to get our attack gear in order, to rest, and to await further orders. Numerous varied troop formations passed by our provisional camp. The orders we awaited never came, but the movement of foot soldiers, artillery, and ammunition wagons went by in a continuous stream throughout the night and all the next day. Two days later we were still observing these columns of people, and moreover, artillery and ammunition pass us by. The fourth day we were finally ordered forward, and at six o'clock in the evening we got underway.

This was, however, not the usual march to the front battle lines. First, we unloaded all of our tools onto materials wagons and then, with the company commander in the lead, we marched one and a half hours in strict tempo. It was only because our commander went with us that we had an idea that something unusual was happening.

We saw things on our road that we had never seen before. We could hardly be in doubt, for there was so much of the military in back of the front. Each kilometer we stumbled upon a new regiment. The woods

The German pioneer company at the Chemins des Dames, January 1918; Artur Boer designated by a white "×" on the right (photographer unknown, but taken with Artur H. Boer's camera).

were sprinkled with artillery, and it seemed like even the open road was filled with loads of shells of various calibers that were being hauled. We did not suspect the main purpose of this entire scene. It was the great turning point in the war against France, the offensive at the Chemin de Dames.

We rested in the protection of our trenches about a kilometer in back of the front lines for about a half hour. At eight o'clock the heavy artillery was to begin the bombardment of the enemy positions. In contrast to the other offensives, we the attacking forces were spread out unprotected all over the map. The hundreds of batteries of heavy 18–30cm guns were grouped together four pieces each. Throughout the night we couldn't think about resting beneath their fire. The projectiles whisked above our heads without cessation, and the general noise of the barrage on the other side was like heavy thunder. Our commanders insured that each man was equipped with gas masks, which were kept in readiness. Additional filters were doled out, and we were told that an enormous gas attack from our side was in progress. We noticed only a few shells that fell from the enemy in answer. The entire thing seemed like it would be overwhelming from our side. During the barrage we were able to go into the reserve trenches. As we passed by a field we observed that the light artillery was being set up; without protection, the batteries stood there in row upon row, truly numbering in the hundreds. Later we learned that the sum was about eight hundred guns which fired only shells with gas in them.

The moment we arrived at the second reserve positions we were divided into three posts as observers, strengthening the machine gun positions with hand grenades. We were to defend them in the case that the enemy unexpectedly attacked during the preparatory barrage. We already knew that directly ahead of us were primarily English forces.

On the opposite side the terrain was heavily built up, which was designated by us as a keyhole, since it looked like that to us. Our military leaders also knew that beneath this keyhole were quarters and extensive bunkers for an appreciable number of troops. We came into contact with the soldiers in the bunker and learned that they had planted a hundred heavy mine throwers at the front. At the end of the barrage they were to cast into the keyhole a hundred heavy mines.

About two o'clock in the night the artillery was enhanced by even heavier pieces. These worked on the forward positions of the opposition.

17. The Marne Offensive

The night trembled in expectation of what would come at the dawn. We had never experienced such a gigantic artillery barrage. At four o'clock in the morning the light artillery began their work, and in the true sense of the word we knew that supernatural forces were at work. We sent over gas and even more gas. These hundred-some-odd field cannons were located only a short distance in back of us. The projectiles whipped by our heads at a height of barely five to eight meters as they passed over our lines. If we looked back all we could see was a single wave of fire from the muzzles. The hot air pressure sickened the atmosphere around us; we could not understand each other than through sign language.

Finally we noticed a detonation in our own front lines and immediately thereafter a horrible sound that shook the earth underneath us. The hundred mines had been cast over and now the sign for the attack was given. This charge was the most bloodless we had ever encountered at the Western Front. We hurriedly hopped out of our positions. We had never before seen our charging troops move forward in such an orderly fashion.

Coming through our own and the enemy's barbed wire to the opposite side without difficulty, we encountered no opposition. A few dead soldiers lay in front of the trench. This was suspicious. At any moment we expected to be met with withering machine gun fire. Soon, however, we passed the front lines, and in the reserve trenches we saw the fruits of our artillery. Everywhere, on the roads, in the trenches, in the bunkers we found masses of dead. On all of these corpses could be seen an unpleasant color in their faces and hands. There weren't many that were buried by the shells, but rather all we could see were those poisoned by German gas. We were forced to put on our gas masks to protect ourselves from our own gas that was left in the area. We were forbidden to sit down, for the gas still remained in the knee-high grass. We were also strictly admonished not to touch any of the enemy's food, which we would otherwise have gladly confiscated. Everything was poisoned.

We came to a road where dead horses lay in a ditch. In front of a bunker there were half-clothed soldiers who had not made it to their place of protection. Everyone had a disturbing color to their faces. It was a terrible sight for us. We could not believe that a gas attack could have such an effect. Some of our own soldiers had to be remanded to our medics, for they could not look upon this scene without sitting down and resting. We marched along an enclosed trench to an English reserve position where artillery batteries were mounted. This too reflected the same scene of men who had been overtaken by a gas attack. Apart from this, we also saw the effect of the German heavy bombardment. Direct hits were especially noticeable in the positions of the heavy artillery of the opposition. I remember a horrible scene there of a human being dissected by a shell. Because the shell had hit the soldier directly in front of a bunker it left the main core of the body as if resting, but the various limbs and head lay strewn about in the vicinity. Despite the fact that we had been accustomed to so much, we were deeply shaken and no one said a word. We moved on to new horrors.

The breakthrough at the Chemin des Dames was in any case fortunate for us. The reports were sent in boastful messages, and the leaders of the army let the triumphal fanfares resound.

Following this last operation a neighboring division was directed to revamp and reorganize the English lines for a German defense. It had been demonstrated that the enemy was ill-equipped for gas warfare, or else this battle would have been less successful. The aforementioned keyhole that had been severely hit was surrounded and many prisoners were taken. These were mostly unarmed troops and a medical unit, which subsequently helped out with the disposal of their dead.

Chapter 18

Attack at the Crozat Canal

During our tour of duty at the front we sappers were not as exposed to the so-called continual fire as, for example, the regular infantry. Therefore we gave even more of our efforts to, and had our nerves frayed by, certain normal operations, such as patrol duty or the laying of barbed wire in no man's land before a charge or hand grenade attack. We were certainly trained for all sorts of military duties, but the sort of construction work that called for building pontoon bridges or attacking across some type of water was not part of this until March 23, 1918, on the Somme River between St. Christ and Tergnier.

This position had been a relatively quiet part of the Somme front until shortly before the great push at the Chemin des Dames. I have no idea how the German army leadership decided to revitalize the front lines there or direct the attention of the enemy away from an area where there would soon be an attack. On March 23rd we undertook a sort of supply muster behind the St. Christ–Tergnier Front. In the afternoon the company was divided into groups designated as battle, storm, and pontoon troops. Myself, I belonged to the ordinance and communications brigade of the battle troop. The communications company had as their task the building of a relay between the storm troopers and division headquarters.

The latter consisted of the commander of the entire troop formation and was about 800 meters behind the attack lines. There were five of us that were ordered to maintain telephone lines between them. We went out with our materials and wires. Our battle group was then divided between five infantry companies. The pontoon company was taken by train to a birch grove where the pontoons were being prepared by the division building corps. When day began to break we laid out our telephone lines from the forward post to a farmhouse where the division had its headquarters. The apparatus was installed and tested, and an extra line as a reserve was laid out in the same direction, although about fifty meters away.

A charge was to be made without artillery preparation, and our front was to be moved to the other side of a canal called "Le Canal de Crozat." In silence the pontoon troop carried the half-pontoons that would be used to as part of the trenches that lay closest to the bank of the canal. The attack was to begin to the left of us, carried out by an infantry regiment and an engineering company from Magdeburg, with whom we often worked together. When we had directed the enemy interest towards this wing, we were to move our reserve battle troops across the canal and complete the movement of the front. At eleven o'clock at night we saw the flare rockets on our left side, and simultaneously a heavy machine gun barrage began. We knew that the assault had started. We didn't hear any artillery fire, and as a consequence we assumed that the troops were fighting hand-to-hand. Across from us the enemy had begun to light up no man's land with flares and directed their artillery toward a wood in back of us and the road which ran beside the farmhouse where our division headquarters lay. It was clear that they did not intend to allow reinforcements to move forward. We who manned the telephones didn't have anything to do at this time other than to test the connection with headquarters. Experience had taught us not to string wire in the vicinity of a road, but rather over free terrain. Thus the lines would be subject to less damage.

Our company had for the most part no long-standing experience with building pontoon bridges, and our thoughts were constantly with those boys. We hoped that they would be able to escape having to use the pontoon bridge. There was the possibility that the troops on the left side, who were already on the other side of the canal, could establish the movement to the front we desired.

The time had arrived for us to spring into action, but the enemy still sent over innumerable flares above us and forced us to lie silent. The officers became nervous. The entire thing was coming apart. Three companies of infantry awaited the signal to go across the canal. Finally, a camouflaged pontoon bridge of birch was successfully put together and with extreme caution brought forward to the canal bank step by

18. Attack at the Crozat Canal

step. The boys were so diligent in getting the bridge into the water that not a splash could be heard.

The infantry gathered in groups in the protection of bushes that grew by the shore and soundlessly made their way across the pontoon bridge. They also succeeded in sending over a heavy machine gun company. Against all of our anticipation, it seemed like this would go well, even though we found ourselves in dangerous proximity to the enemy. The area on the other side of the canal was the most advantageous for those troops who were able to cross. The entire place was so overgrown with bushes that it gave excellent shelter to the soldiers. We didn't notice any movement by the enemy on the other side. Of course, we heard numerous machine gun salvos directed at us, but these went over our heads. Soon we were to learn that the enemy did not consider that we would attack just here, for they had no artillery in this sector.

In the far right distance we saw the muzzle fire from a battery, and the next moment four shells whistled overhead to hit in back of our front lines. There was a certain nervousness among our boys at the sound of these projectiles. But the commanders restored order and the movement of the troops continued. For safety's sake we took off our backpacks in case the pontoon bridge would be damaged. This circumstance was later to prove most fortunate. Some of the older reservists, among them a rather calm man from the Baltic coast, took over the directing of the pontoons, and it seemed like everything was going well. Those of us in the communications company were close to the canal and had the task of informing the general staff of the progress of the operation. The battle on the left side of the front continued apace. Reports from there reached us only sporadically, but there too all seemed to be going according to calculations.

A great portion of the infantry had already crossed the canal, and the solders began to dig in. Suddenly, the noise of an airplane could be heard. Despite the darkness of night, the French flew over the battle zone. Now everything became much more critical for us. Simultaneously the enemy's illumination of the battle zone was intensified, and thus we were put in the dangerous situation of being discovered. The artillery from the enemy flank became much more active, and the bombardment of our positions became heavier. Our boys worked on ferrying the cargo without reacting to it. Soon we calculated that all of the troops would be across, but then it happened; two of the pontoon ferries had emptied their cargo and were coming back across. They were in the middle when four shells hit in between them. One sprang a leak from a piece of shrapnel and sank, while another listed. Each of the ferries carried four men—all in all eight soldiers—of which only three made it. These swam to the shore. Then we heard a voice: "Help me, I'm trapped." It was the fellow from the Baltic who was holding on to a bush that dragged the water. Some of the other fellows helped him get up, and it was then that we saw that both his legs were riddled with shrapnel. We immediately took him in hand, but no matter how much we attempted to stop the blood, it didn't help and he died before he could be transported out. We stopped the fleet for a moment when the fire became too intense. We led a few men along with ammunition over on the flotation devices, and then we prepared the defense on the other side of the canal.

The troops who had landed on the other side received orders to remain passive, because the enemy had still not discovered the situation. The next day, in the light of dawn, the neighboring troops from the left arrived, and together they built up new positions. The quite weak enemy positions directly in front were then stormed with the help of our artillery, thus keeping the French in check between St. Christ and Tergnier.

After the taking of the positions on the other side of the Crozat canal the French began to concentrate on the terrain in back of the lines, and the farmhouse where the division staff had their quarters came under heavy assault. We had established telephone connections with other regiments stationed in the foremost lines, including a Bavarian assault battalion. We received news from them that the enemy's position was weak and that we could continue to drive the enemy past his own battle lines. Like the Bavarians, our division still did not have any orders to continue the offensive, but we expected them at any time.

The opposition's artillery fire became much stronger during the day and was directed exclusively at the headquarters behind the front. Owing to that we found what we most feared had happened, the telephone connection with headquarters had been broken.

At seven o'clock in the morning important news from the front arrived and an hour before that we sent out the last of the messages. Now it was our turn to run off to the farmhouse where the headquarters lay. Of course, we took with us the material needed to reconnect our

18. Attack at the Crozat Canal

lines. But it was truly work in vain, considering how broken they were. Moreover, we couldn't receive any messages from staff headquarters, for they had to maintain other numerous connections. One of our officers, Lieutenant Fürster, whose position was as adjutant to the main commander of the sappers working with headquarters, arrived with the orders that we had to re-establish the telephone connections whatever the circumstances. He himself would come along to ensure that our reports, which had earlier been sent to headquarters, had indeed arrived. Comrade Studt, our most senior telephone operator, and I took with us telephones and the apparatus that would find where the lines were cut, and the three of us set off. The closer we came to headquarters, the shorter the exposed lengths of line, until our own lines were not the only ones exposed on the ground; rather, there were many others so that we were able to find the connections to a plethora of other German troop formations.

Twenty meters before we came to the staff headquarters was a small grove that we had to pass. Within we saw a newly-arrived ammunition wagon that had been shot to pieces. One of the men was dead and a second, wounded in the head, wandered aimlessly around in the bushes. We took care of the wounded, bandaged him, and showed him the way to the nearest ambulance. Studt and the lieutenant went up to the dead horses, and the latter thought that fresh meat would be a change, whereupon Studt took out his bayonet to cut a piece out of the horses hind quarters. This was at least his intention, but he was prevented by the officer. In the next instant shrapnel pierced the air from shell that winged its way over us towards the farmhouse.

For thirty seconds we expected a barrage of projectiles and immediately ran to our goal. At the headquarters everything was in motion. It was decided to move it to a more protected place. The staff headquarters was far too exposed to shelling, and it was not beyond believing that the enemy had discovered its existence. This was not so extraordinary, because so many went in and out despite the proximity of the shelling. The enemy air corps did not remain inactive either. But before they could move, a shell landed in the courtyard and killed two riding horses. After consultation with the staff communications officers, we moved the entire post about two hundred meters behind the woods in order to construct a new station and re-establish communication with the battle lines. Because it was impossible to splice the shot-up lines, we laid new wires on poles two meters higher than those we laid in the woods. However, new orders arrived at the division for the troops to move to the village of St. Christ that had just been taken by the infantry. This became a long road. First, we couldn't move as an entire company, and second, in order to avoid the enemy's reach we had to detour by way of a road five kilometers longer. Later in the day we arrived at this aforementioned village, which was in rather awful shape from shelling, and immediately we built defensive foxholes for we suspected some sort of retaliation from the enemy by the evening.

Evening fell, but the French kept quiet. Lacking any support we spent the night with the infantry and prepared a camp up against the walls of the village churchyard. We positioned the supply wagon and kitchen behind the churchyard in the protection of an old and tall tree. In the foxholes that were barely half a meter deep and protected by a dirt mound, we established only a watch post, expecting eventually to be overrun. But instead of the anticipated attack, the enemy began too engulf the village itself and the churchyard in artillery fire. In the church, which lay a bit further off, a temporary field hospital had been established, and the medical personnel had their hands full with work. The field kitchen had been able to cook food for the company, and prior to the evening attack we also received coffee. The night was cold, and we didn't get much rest.

We were allowed to go get more coffee to warm us up, and therefore we crept over the churchyard to the field kitchen. On this occasion some of us noticed huge stone slabs in the churchyard that had been shot to pieces. We investigated these further and found that they had served to cover family graves. We assumed that there were also newly-dug or empty graves. This was correct. When we looked closer at them and saw that they formed a walled grotto two meters deep with so-called niches for caskets on each side. Someone said that these would make excellent bunks for us for the night. The idea spread and was accepted. There were many graves that were not yet in use, and without further discussion these were appropriated by as many as could fit. The boys lay in these holy holes the entire night not only against the cold but also whatever shelling came our way. When the company commander asked about the night quarters of the soldiers the next morning, his subordinates replied laconically that if the boys wished at this time to prepare a rather nice burial for themselves, they weren't going to gainsay it.

Chapter 19

The Argonne, 1918

Following an interminable moving about, we found ourselves in a part of France where the Germans didn't have a chance of advancing, having maintained their positions in place since the beginning of the war. This was the Argonne between the Meuse and Aisne rivers. My first impression of this chain of mountains was overwhelming. I simply could not understand that human beings would make such a place of natural beauty a stage for war. And yet the deep valleys echoed with the bursting of shells. But despite four years of battle in the same area none of the evil of mankind could destroy nature and the magnificent beauty that the mountains offered in their majesty.

Here in the Argonne both the French and the Germans each occupied their respective mountain ridges. The trenches were buttressed and well-built, and thus were difficult to approach. Here the troops had reinforced their positions during the years. The chances of making any forward progress here were equally great or small. It was trench warfare in the true sense of the word. Here it depended solely upon the inventive abilities of the enemy to deal out some sort of blow at the weaker points. But these were few, and the troops remained dug in where they were.

Trenches were constructed by means of explosives and digging in zigzag fashion in the cleared areas. These were carefully camouflaged with large nets made of steel wire. In these were erected barriers that blocked the insides from view. Because of the difficult conditions at the front we had to carry everything that was needed in the bunkers by way of these trenches on an almost daily basis. This was a refreshing task, depending upon the burned-out paths. The French artillery shelled the trenches without cessation using canister shells. Any sort of fire using regular shells was not possible for either opponent due to the short distance between the lines.

Observations were done by airplane reconnaissance and the long sausage-like observation balloons, which were up in the air day and night. The transportation of supplies we did mostly by night, for we had to find our way over empty ground in order to avoid the narrow trenches. But the utmost caution was necessary, and none of us were allowed to smoke. Even the slightest glimmer of light in the terrain would call down upon us an entire salvo of artillery. It was sometimes difficult at times when we had to help transport the sick or wounded to the rear. Such transportation was particularly painful on the narrow paths.

An agreement between the French and ourselves had been worked out equally so that on certain roads in the valleys the wounded could be transferred in broad daylight to hospitals behind the front. They did, however, have to be accompanied by a visible Red Cross flag. We were thankful for this agreement, but unfortunately once there occurred a catastrophe despite this knowledge.

One day a troop of twenty men who were slightly wounded during a hand grenade attack arrived at our position. We didn't have a Red Cross flag of the agreed upon dimensions at hand, we asked that our comrades wait until one of the medics could obtain one. They were of the opinion that this would take too long. They insisted upon continuing on immediately. Perhaps their wounds were far more serious than we knew. After some consultation, we allowed them to go, but we made them aware that they were setting themselves up to be in danger of coming under fire. Regardless, the medic made for each and every one of them a white piece of paper with the information on their wounds, pinned it to their clothing, and they were allowed to go. We didn't hear anything more about them. A few days later, one of the Red Cross wagons was making its way to the field hospital when it serendipitously found the twenty men on a hillock. All were dead, having been hit by machine gun fire from an enemy aviator.

We had also known for some time that there was also difficult transportation work to be done in the Argonne. Now we were ordered to move into position and work with our infantry. There was little possibility of troop movements within the trenches. Sporadic machine gun fire from various directions, small arms fire from rifle shells, and one

19. The Argonne, 1918

or another medium sized mines, these were the everyday occurrences and not particularly dangerous. One could protect oneself from these weapons, for they were visible for the most part. Sometimes a French aviator would fly in and drop a small bomb, but if one kept an eye out, it was easy to find protection in time. As mentioned before, the trenches were solid and carved into the mountains. But inside the mountains was something new and interesting with which we were to become acquainted.

All of the front line duty above ground in the Argonne was a stalemate during the work, but underneath the movement of both sides was all the more lively. It was here that the hopeless competition for points took place. All of the work that occurred here was like the digging by miners in a coal mine. The only difference was that one was not after coal or ore, but rather one carried on the work with huge amounts of explosives so that such work could undermine the enemy. From a technical standpoint, it was the job of the commanders to figure out how

The sapper company at work in the Argonne in 1918 (photograph by Artur H. Boer; van Boer family archives).

and where one could direct a blow at the weakest point of the enemy positions.

In order to advance to the enemy and under his forward positions, numerous methods were used. From the first trench a shaft was dug until one advanced beneath the valley path; this had to be a tunnel of considerable depth in order to protect it from shell hits. Then the tunnel continued towards the mountainside. This began to climb again. If the calculations were correct, one would then find themselves underneath the enemy trenches. There a room called a "cavern" in miner's language was built. This could be quite large, depending upon how deep under the enemy one found oneself and subsequently also how much dynamite had to be used. And then? One needs not hazard much of a guess!

How simple it is to describe this underground work, if one takes the time to think about it, for it was the result of the soldiers' patient work day and night, regardless of the season. And now it was our turn to continue this work with the help of the infantry. This construction required many people. But what would we do with all of the stone and earth that we dug up? In a continual line the soldiers carried out in sandbags everything up to the light of day and emptied it behind the trenches. Often we felt sorry for ourselves. This was slave labor. But if we thought this was rough, we considered that others might have it worse. And thus we continued. There were many places in this part of the front where one did this sort of work simultaneously. The way down into the mine tunnels and shafts was about twenty to twenty-five meters deep. When we succeeded in getting a tunnel and explosive chamber ready, the latter was filled with as much dynamite as had been calculated, and this was nothing to sneeze at. To use five hundred kilograms of dynamite was nothing special.

If underneath the ground we felt ourselves safe from bullets and shells, we were not always certain that we were without peril. It happened in our company one time that, during a short pause in our work, we heard tapping in the ground from the enemy side. Of course, it was only natural that the opponents were doing the same sort of work against our positions. Our observations were reported and we were told to break off the job. Instead, we mounted a microphone in the tunnel with a wire leading up to the trenches. Now we listened the entire time and determined that the enemy really was at work in proximity to us.

19. The Argonne, 1918

This was heard for a long time by a guard post, but suddenly all sound ceased. Two of our boys now received orders to investigate the situation carefully and see what happened to the microphone. When too much time had passed for the return of the boys, a couple of others went down into the shaft. These soon came back and said that the first group must have fainted due to the gas that lay in a pool at the bottom of the hole. We suspected that the enemy knew how close we were. They had broken through and taken the microphone, and then filled the tunnel with carbon dioxide gas. Several men equipped with gas masks fetched the boys, and they immediately were put in the care of doctors and taken to the hospital. The shaft was immediately filled with explosives and detonated.

The strange thing about explosions on the Argonne Front was that losses were not as high as one might have thought. The stalemate at the front allowed equal chances for both the Germans and French, and the result was that explosions were carried out by both sides daily at a specific hour. This worked like a sort of agreement to spare human lives. If, for example, we detonated at five o'clock in the morning, which we usually did, we could expect a detonation from the opposition two hours later. This observation taught us to leave the deep protective chambers at a certain time. Seldom did one witness an explosion in the bunkers themselves.

The Argonne Front was therefore only an immobile station for troops who came here from more dangerous positions exhausted and in need of a bit of rest. We too were ready to march onward again after a month. The guesses about our next place on the front were many, but as usual this was kept secret so that even the officers themselves could only tell us after a long time into the march. This time we went northwards. The guesses among us were that this meant the front in Flanders.

Chapter 20

The Red Baron

We did not, however, go to Flanders, but rather we had an opportunity to make an acquaintance with the English. This was at the Noyon-Mont Didier front, which needed strengthening from numerous troops with technical capability. After a short railway journey we underwent a really tiresome march of three miles on a road paved with stone that led from Cambrai to the front at Bapaume. The apparent calm behind the front was contrasted by the attacks at close quarters between the battling forces around the little village of Bapaume.

The most unusual thing about this for us was that, in contrast to the other fronts, the enemy ignored all troop movements behind the lines despite many of their own observation balloons, which could overlook the terrain for many miles. Even the reserve trenches were not shelled with any frequency. On the other hand the artillery fire directed at those closest was ferocious. This resulted in bitter close-quarters fighting, the outcome of which was that the trenches could be occupied by the English and Germans many times each day. The number of dead was certainly not great, but masses of wounded would come from there, and it was difficult to fill the gaps in the defense on an equal basis. It was, however, not the ground battle that was all determining here, but rather the fighting in the skies. Nowhere else on the entire Western Front was it so lively as in the aerial battles as the Bapaume front. Here, the German pilot, [Manfred] von Richthofen, along with his squadron, were active in the skies. The appellation "The Red Baron" came about because Richthofen had painted his airplane completely red.

From the earliest time of the morning until late at night there was a terrible activity in the skies above us. Our eyes were directed upwards

20. The Red Baron

towards the firmament, whatever time of day it was. If one heard machine gun patter, one looked up first and foremost at the smaller cloud formations. The Red Baron kept himself hidden in back of these in order to swoop down like a hawk on the opposition. Richthofen showed a singular cold-bloodedness, but in every battle that we observers saw, the English aviators were brave and refused to give in until the very last. But it was Richthofen and his men who most often won with their battle tactics. Sometimes we heard machine guns barking for an extended time high above the clouds until suddenly a machine dropped down through the clouds. And on this front, it was seldom German.

The English were rather industrious fliers. But however high they flew, one of Richthofen's boys flew higher still and shredded them like cabbage. Late one morning, we were engaged in building a bunker in the second reserve line when we heard the clatter of several machine guns high above us. The weather was magnificent, and the air clear in the sunshine. It was almost unthinkable that an air battle would take place. But nonetheless we saw at about seven hundred meters high two small cloud specks, and it was towards these that we directed our attention immediately. We were not able at that time to discern any machine. After about five minutes a plane came spiraling down through a cloud. We followed its out of control descent towards the ground with our eyes. But at about two hundred meters it righted itself and flew on a direct course towards the German lines. It was an Englishman. We saw nothing of the German machine. We then heard the new sound of weapons fire further off on our side, and three German machines appeared, flying lower than the Englishman on their way to the front. But the Englishman, secure in the advantage that his height gave him, did not alter course, but rather continued onwards until the German anti-aircraft batteries call a halt to him. With respect to maneuverability, the little machine could climb faster than the larger German planes. After a few salvos from his machine guns, he climbed to a higher altitude and returned to his course towards the front. His task was apparently to observe and not to engage in any dogfight. But when the Englishman was well on his way to nearing the battle lines, a small German machine appeared as if conjured and cut him off. Now a graceful dance began between them. Each one tried to get above the other, and with each change in position could be heard intensive fire from their weapons. Soon it seemed that both fought only as two small specks, but one of them had to go down eventually, which we duly recognized. Something flat spiraled down close to us. It was a large piece of the English machine shot full of holes. We still could follow the maneuvers above. It seemed like the artillery all over the front observed the drama, as it was so silent on this occasion. Among those of us who were used to such various displays, we discussed the battle in a lively manner, but I never heard the statement that it was the German machine that ought to win. We marveled at both opponents equally for their attacks. Eventually the Englishman came down in a spin, but this time it wasn't a deliberate maneuver. The German followed him closely in a tight aerial dance in order not to lose his victim. But already before he could pull his machine up, the Englishman lost a wing and fell to the earth like a stone. Richthofen's aviator—the German was one of his squadron—circled a few times over the crash site of the other plane and disappeared again.

There were quite honorable manners in these aerial battles, and we often observed that when a squadron encountered a single enemy aviator, only one of the planes undertook the battle against his opponent. We positioned our observations balloons about one or two miles behind the battle trenches. These waived like large sausages at a height of about two hundred meters and were fastened by means of steel cables to a machine that regulated their position in the air, as well as raising and lower them on the command of the observer. In the beginning, many were shot down by the enemy's pilots. The reason was that the machinery functioned too slowly or that there were not enough defenses on the ground. In these cases, the occupant jumped down with a parachute. But later we mounted fast-firing so-called flak guns (anti-aircraft cannon) whose every tenth shell was filled with magnesium, and new orders for raising and lowering the balloon were given, making it difficult for the enemy to come close to these important observation posts. But this or that clever aviator managed to sneak up in the protection of a cloud and destroyed the balloon by means of a fire bomb that spewed burning fuel over its target. Whether or not this pilot succeeded, he could be certain that he would then become involved in a dogfight.

We were quartered in a cottage in a little village. The artillery had raised a new battery of unusual construction in the courtyard. About the village were mounted three anti-aircraft guns to protect the battery

20. The Red Baron

from unwelcome aviators. The secret about this battery was that it shot shells of normal field size twice the usual distance. The order to fire was given only at night, and the field personnel could take it quite easy since the enemy did not seek out batteries so far behind the front. But during the firing we heard an English plane above us. (Our ears were already trained to differentiate between the engines of the various countries.) That night nothing happened, but in the light of the next day a small machine appeared out of a cloud at top speed shooting like lightning, did a quick turn about twenty meters overhead and quickly disappeared. Obviously the battery position had been detected by the enemy, for this meant the peace of the village was now ended. The same evening the village was subjected to a heavy fire from the enemy, and we troops had to seek other quarters.

I remember an event that happened on a Sunday morning. Our platoon had been at the front the entire night before and was going to rest during the day. Of course, we had the usual day orders, personal hygiene and the mustering for proclamations and news. We were standing in the courtyard when we were surprised by an English observation plane. Our supply wagons were neatly parked not far from us and badly camouflaged. The pilot was observant enough and threw out a couple of small bombs which didn't cause any real damage. An anti-aircraft gun blasted away a few shots without result.

But then we discovered two large German biplanes at a fortuitous height. If the Englishman was interested in what he saw or if stupidity simply took over, he nonchalantly ignored these large machines and circled continuously above us at a great height. We would naturally have sought shelter if the circumstances had allowed it. One German plane made a turn towards the front and then turned about in order to cut off the escape of the Englishman. The most remarkable thing for us was that anti-aircraft guns held their fire. Suddenly it began to rain bullets from above. This duel lasted a long time. The other German plane now began to draw closer to the Englishman and moved in a circular pattern above him. This was clearly an attempt to force him down. Time and time again the little Englishman attempted to get above his antagonist, shooting industriously all the while. But at last we observed that the Englishman must have been wounded, for the maneuvering of his machine became more deliberate. He still fired a salvo into the air at an altitude of fifty meters. Then the aircraft made a turn downwards, which actually looked like a perfect landing. But during the landing in a field the plane hit a telephone pole and stopped almost undamaged. We didn't have far to go to the landing place, but we didn't dare to approach the plane, for it occurred to us that an unhurt or lightly wounded pilot would defend himself even on the ground in order not to be taken prisoner. Both of the Germans had taken off, and we carefully went over to the English plane. There sat a young man barely twenty years of age dead at the stick. He had been shot through the foot, but the mortal shot went through his neck. I have to admit that this made us sad for the young, brave boy.

We experienced another instance of heroic feats on the German side one summer afternoon at Soissons in France. There was a large aircraft of an English type, a two-seater. The armament consisted of two heavy machine guns and a thirty millimeter moveable piece of the type the English used extensively in Flanders. We were on a march and rested during the night in a little village in northern France. The next day, before we continued the march, we heard above us a large machine at about a thousand meters. It was rather rare to find such a large aircraft flying all alone. Normally they were escorted by smaller fighters. But it wasn't too many minutes before we heard a commotion up there. A small German biplane was after the large machine. The Englishmen used their automatic guns industriously, but the German, just like a furious wasp, thoroughly worked over the other plane. Thanks to the fact that the German could more easily maneuver in his little machine, the large aircraft received machine gun fire from all directions before it could alter course. The distance between them was not great, and we had the impression that the Englishmen had to be blown away. But we already anticipated that the Englishmen wouldn't last long in this intensive barrage that the German unleashed mainly from above. This was indeed the case. Soon there came a heavy black smoke from the English plane, which indicated that the oil had caught fire. In our opinion, the battle could no longer continue. But despite their difficult condition, the Englishmen seemed to continue to fire without letting up, and the German didn't let them go either. The larger plane began to lose considerable altitude and now found itself about a hundred meters in the sky. We clearly heard the drum of the engines, and saw a long tail of fire trailed after the machine. The most remarkable thing was that the pilot still continued to use his machine guns, and we didn't

20. The Red Baron

notice anything wrong with the plane's steering mechanism. The battle had lasted a full twelve minutes, and we calculated that it had been two minutes since the fire had started. Certainly, we had often seen machines on fire, but these immediately crashed to the ground. It was really inconceivable that this Englishman could maintain himself in flight with a burning engine. Finally, the machine glided to a perfect landing in a field about a half kilometer from us and burned. Naturally, we who had seen the duel ran to the crash site. The German aviator, a major from Württemberg, also landed about eight hundred meters from the burning plane and came forward. When the still burning wreckage calmed a bit, we dragged the severely-burned men out. The corpses were clothed in thick leather coverings, and we took their identification from the pockets of their underclothing. They were a major and a captain. The German pilot took charge of the papers and identification and asked the officer present for a written description of this final battle. This was partially for the merit list of the aviators and partly for the permanent exchange of identification that existed for each flying machine shot down. The major certainly had done enough to win the prize, but for us the admiration for the brave Englishmen was greater.

Chapter 21

The Offensive at the Marne

The largest but also the last breakthrough on the Western Front occurred on the heights of the Chemin des Dames. Now the Germans were on an unstoppable offensive. The infantry and artillery pursued the combined French and English troops. Every forward attack from the Germans was done with such surprise that there was no time to prepare the people living behind the front for an orderly flight. We came to villages where carts with the most necessary possession loaded by the refugees stood in front of the houses. There were masses of baggage piled onto the platforms at the railway stations. At a military airfield a plane stood ready to take off, but the pilot lay on the ground shot.

It was about noon in a larger village. Everywhere in the houses the tables were laid for lunch. Food ready to eat stood on the stoves, and in many cases it began to burn during the cooking. In one farm house they were not able to move an old women lying in a bed, but the soldiers passing through had ransacked the house looking for clothing. In front of a house lay a young woman shot through the head. In the garden a man had hung himself in a tree. In his pocket was found a paper upon which it was written: "Two times the German soldiers have stolen my possessions; I will not live through a third." For us soldiers this was viewed with sorrow.

We belonged to the Seventh Reserve Division and had to be prepared close to the rear of the attacking forces. Sometimes there could be a lull in the offensive attack, and we had the possibility of resting as well. And during these pauses we were able to see how the soldiers that came after from the various companies moved about in the newly occupied places.

The enemy had well-stocked supply depots behind the front. I had

21. The Offensive at the Marne

occasion to see one of them. There were sacks with peas, beans, corn and flour, but not all of the sacks were full. Everyone was cut open, and one could wade through the stuff that flowed out from them. The pantries were torn down, and bread and preserves lay strewn about. It was a scandal that we had to consider that our own countrymen had done this.

We found ourselves in one of the most fruitful wine regions in France. Wine was found in every cellar, and of course the military was rather eager to taste this magnificence. As drunkenness took hold, discipline vanished, but there was a looting of civil property without parallel. The wine cellars were the most sought after, and holes were chopped into the large barrels where the people stored their everyday wine, the so-called "cider." Thus the cellars were filled foot deep with wine. The most insane thing I saw was in a shed in a farm house where the French military orchestra must have had their quarters. In the loft could be found a complete group of brass instruments. But some idiot had put up a ladder and pounded all of these expensive instruments flat. In a more expensive house belonging to a lawyer I saw the finest furniture, but virtually all of it was broken to pieces. The sheets and blankets were strewn about, and the linen closet was empty. An apparently expensive piano was totally smashed to bits. This caused great pain for a music lover. In another house the soldiers had set a table, and after having dinner, they gathered up all of the dishes and silverware in the tablecloth, just like a sack, and threw it into a corner of the room. I saw innumerable smashed mirrors. In short, I have never seen a more vandalized culture in the enemy country. The German military leaders were not able to teach their soldiers better to respect French property.

During the war years there was a lack of metal in Germany. Therefore, the order came to take down all church bells in the occupied French villages. These bells were then sent to Germany for melting down. I was with a division that received the order to take down the only bell in the village church. The protests by the mayor, the village manager, were in vain, and we set to work. To lower the bell offered some difficulties in the narrow tower. We were then ordered to blow it down. We bound dynamite to the steeple, lit it, and the bell fell to earth.

In another place in France all of the copper and brass pipes in a brewery were to be disassembled. These were loaded onto freight cars for further transport to Germany by rail. All of this can only be expressed by the designation "marauders in a foreign country."

Chapter 22

French Tank Attack

In the late summer of 1918 we had once again returned to a position between the Meuse and the Argonne. This was one of our most common places, one to which we were often posted. Of course, this position meant trenches, bunkers, foxholes, and reinforced field positions. If I would speak of the place where the engineers lived, it would be a question of circumstances. But it is not the intention to show the conditions where one lay and slept. It is more important to tell about the events along the front. I will only comment that during the war our company lived in the strangest and most variable quarters. Not even the most lively imagination can conceive them: tents and bunks thrown together from stones and bits of rope, in holes in the ground, and in pre-fabricated barracks, in stalls for horses and dikes, in ruins, and, as I have already mentioned, in mausoleums in a French churchyard. But here between Meuse and the Argonne we arrived at a real holiday resort, as we usually called such places. It was a beech forest with well-appointed barracks built of logs. There were even plants. We were quite at home there, and sometimes it was difficult to believe that it was a war camp. It was a calm and peaceful place, and only from a distance could we hear the weak sounds of the front. Here a commissary and an officer's and enlisted man's mess had been set up. But at the front, which lay five kilometers from this camp, we carried out our usual work, stringing barbed wire, laying mines, and night patrol, not to mention guard duty.

In my descriptions can often be found periods of stagnation during the war, which we named a *Sitzkrieg*. It is odd that no one really speaks about this subject. But no matter how often we came to such a front, our tension and watchfulness were none the less for it. Even at the calmest front it was a matter of life or death for an individual. Here the

22. French Tank Attack

Impromptu musical group of the German pioneer company; Artur Boer with his violin on the left (photographer unknown, but taken with Artur H. Boer's camera; van Boer family archives).

dangers were more hidden for us, more suppressed than an open attack by any one side. I have seen many of my comrades wounded or killed during the war, and I could perhaps paint the most horrible scenes in the most vivid colors. Here I only wish to say that, after three years on the front, I had acquired experience; we missed our fallen comrades, which increased our suffering from a psychological point of view.

As active as the enemy was along the Siegfried Front, where the German forces retreated step by step, meter by meter, it was all the more quiet here. The French were opposite us, and between Meuse and the Argonne we had not yet perceived any restlessness. But this situation could not last for long. One speaks of the calm before the storm, and six days later we experienced it.

On September 25th all hell broke loose on this front as well. Already during the evening of the twenty-fifth we received warning of the enemy's intentions from French pickets. The attack was thought out in grand style, and the artillery fire began in full strength about two o'clock in the morning. Despite this barrage the Germans gathered together their defensive troops, and I remember how we ran through the glens and through the mountains towards the front with our attack packs in pitch black night. We were successful in attaining the first battle trenches without casualties. There we awaited the enemy attack. The barrage was not answered by our side, and our company had to stay unsupported in the trench to defend it. We were divided into platoons under the command of their respective officers. Our defensive weapons consisted mainly of hand grenades and the so-called anti-tank gun. This was almost three times larger than the usual weapon, and the ammunition was much bigger and made of steel instead of the usual lead used by the normal projectiles. The striking strength was calculated to pierce eight millimeters of tank armor. Apart from the size, this weapon was difficult to handle.

During the time that we expected the French would attack, those who did not have guard duty spent the time in the bunker. We played cards, read, or spoke with each other in order to relieve a certain nervousness. There were also guys with gallows humor who knew the art of encouraging their comrades in such a precarious situation. From time to time we learned what was going on from the guards. About four o'clock in the morning an artillery observer came and set up his telephone apparatus in the bunker. The enemy had begun to direct his fire towards the forward trenches, and the posts were reduced but relieved every quarter hour. The chief officer of the platoon came and made sure that each group was equipped with signal flares. We were to use them if we had to retreat from an enemy attack to signal our artillery where we were. We sappers were the ones who had to cover the retreat during the defense.

At five-thirty the fire diminished at the front line and was directed a little further back towards the reserve. This was the sign that made us ready. The boxes with hand grenades were moved closer to the exit of the bunker to have them at hand, and we prepared each other for the various positions that we needed to occupy. A few minutes before six a post reported that the enemy had fired signal rockets. It was time for us to take our places. The trenches were rather shot up. The infantry placed their machine guns. We went off ourselves to the enfiladed positions at the front lines. Still, our side didn't let fly a single shot. We heard many of our pilots above us. They were there to direct our

22. French Tank Attack

artillery fire towards the attackers. From the enemy side we heard the typical sound of approaching tanks, but we still didn't see them. The pilots gave their signals with varicolored rockets, and the artillery began an intensive barrage with 15 centimeter howitzers. The field artillery engaged in a withering fire with explosive shells and to the right of us the machine gun nests were in full action. Now we saw the first of the tanks poke up over a rise just in front of us. Their speed wasn't especially great. They could only do about 25–30 kilometers per hour. We prepared to shoot our heavy weapons, but at such a distance we still didn't believe we'd get any good result. But then we observed that a number of French soldiers followed behind the tank, and now the firing began with machine guns instead. The artillery observer who was nearby had a good view and directed the light artillery straight in to the enemy's attack formation. But the attackers in the tanks also used their machine guns vigorously. The situation for those of us in the foremost position wasn't great, and we only waited for the traveling marvel to come a bit closer. We had only a vague idea how we were to fight these tanks effectively when they came in range. We could of course use our anti-tank weapons industriously, but these heavy weapons could only be loaded with one shell at a time, and therefore we had to make every shot count. Machine guns were of no use whatsoever against an attacking tank.

There were four sappers and three regular infantry in our front line position. It was well-camouflaged, and we still hadn't been discovered. We discussed whether it would be better to lie on open ground to await the enemy with our weapons. We entertained the thought for a bit that so many of us in such a little hole could all be killed at one time. Suddenly the tank was hit by a shell and its movement ceased. The treads were damaged. Our artillery observer let out a happy shout: "Now boys, we're going to make mincemeat of that thing there." With that he directed the fire to make the attacker completely helpless. But we didn't count on the machine gun that the enclosed tank crew began to use. The entire side stood like a broad dinner table right in front of us at barely a hundred meters distance. It was easy for us to continue firing at this target, but the thought that a single shell from the enemy could make mincemeat of us when our position was discovered kept us from being forced to shoot. Rather, we let the artillery take care of the matter.

The enemy's fire was not directed more towards our line, but one of our infantrymen was wounded. Our platoon sergeant arrived with a few infantrymen with him, indicating that we should follow him. Many of the attacking tanks to the left of us had been taken out of the battle by our artillery, but according to our aerial observers many other rolling fortresses were on the move. Under the leadership of the officer, we moved a distance away to the left wing. There the remainder of our platoon was already at work on a project behind the battle lines. This was to build the so-called tank traps quickly.

We had learned that to build a tank trap took time, and the thought of fulfilling this task in the middle of a ferocious battle gave us pause. But orders had been given for it, and we set to work. Fortunately, the terrain was so well designed so that it could be possible. A pit, like an old mine head, was the most appropriate to use. The side of this pit was oriented towards the front and due to a horrific fire was about three meters lower, but we nonetheless dug an even deeper pit in the middle of the equally burned out road.

We weren't the only ones to undertake such work. A bit further off to the left, our entire Fourth Company was also similarly occupied. These were pitfalls that we only provisionally approved after completion, for the materials themselves (strong tree trunks for the road) were missing, but these were nonetheless proven to be effective. There were no less than five French tanks stuck in these pits. Their occupants had no possibility of defending themselves any longer and were taken prisoner.

From the point of view of the enemy, the entire attack could be called a failure, and the number of prisoners was significant. But experience had taught us that the French would not give up even after such a first failure. The evening fell after a hot day of battle, bringing a well-meaning peace over the front. But the enemy was on his guard. Huge numbers of brilliant rockets arose into the air from the other side, illuminating no man's land. After our defensive work during the day we were given a moment to rest, but all of a sudden order came for the gathered company to work in three shifts in the trenches throughout the night. The defensive bunkers were completely shot to pieces after the day's fighting, and instead we had to dig hastily small bunkers for the infantry. We worked industriously on the small rooms in the trenches, none of which could contain more than four people. The very

22. French Tank Attack

same night the redoubts were equipped with a machine gun company, with one gun in each one. As we immediately recognized, this was what one did for defensive work here on the English front.

When we had made a few crypts for ourselves, we could take it easy. We sat and shared what we had left of the day's rations, and although we were extremely tired, no one sought to relax; rather, we made small talk. One of us, it was our first telephone operator Studt, said, "I wonder how many Frenchmen were lost today. There really are quite a number of dead out there. One might even say that it smells officially like blood." Only later did we reflect on these words when terrible fate chose comrade Studt as one of the many victims of war.

We finally thought we could rest a bit, for no one knew what the coming day had on tap. We hung a tent canvas at the entrance to our bunker and lit a candle stump in order to prepare a miserable camp for ourselves. But this did not work. A courier came and asked for the company telephone operator. Studt immediately packed up his things and both he and I, as reserve operator, followed after the courier. He led us back through the trenches to a bunker where the company commander and doctor were quartered. From here we were to lay a temporary line to our other pioneer company that lay off to the left of us. We were to organize a relay post halfway there that would be manned by one member of each company.

To unreel the line was not pleasant work in the dark. Added to that was the problem that the wires were at the supply wagon, which was somewhere in the vicinity. There we had left all of our telephone equipment. We weren't able to determine where we were, despite the map sketch made by the captain, for we had been in at least ten positions during the last day on this front. But in the hope of finding some soldiers somewhere who could show us the correct way, for we more or less knew the name of the various bits of ground, we moved on out. This was, as we said, to be a temporary line, but this telephone line and this night's work would remain with me for life.

Our company supply chief who was in charge of the supply wagon was to be found in the vicinity of a road. Before we encountered this highway we passed by all sorts of foxholes that were more or less shot to pieces. The enemy was more restless on this sector of the front, and we had to protect ourselves from the occasional shell during this rather difficult duty. Eventually we arrived at the highway and thought we had arrived at the place where the supply wagon was parked. But there were only a few bushes and a shot-up wagon with a number of dead horses. Suddenly a company of soldiers from one of our infantry regiments arrived.

Now we knew where we could obtain our equipment, and soon we arrived and packed up our spools. Then it was a matter of finding the Fourth Company, where we needed to go. After hitting the dirt to avoid the withering fire, we finally arrived and received aid from the men of Company Four. We decided to erect the relay post on the highway from whence we had come.

Underneath an old tree we dug a hole and installed the dry cell batteries, before departing in different directions. Myself and two of my comrades went off towards our company. About five hundred meters from our goal the enemy began to shoot. From the way they landed we knew that they were gas shells. This turned out to be correct. Now we were forced to continue with masks on our faces, which made it all the more difficult. We could not make ourselves be understood for a single word, but rather we were forced to work in close quarters with each other in the dark, using sign language. But at last we arrived at company headquarters, set up the apparatus, and tested the lines to the relay post. This functioned clearly and without static. We relieved the relay station every other hour.

The time was almost five in the morning, when the enemy began to rake the foremost bunkers with a ferocious fire. Orders immediately went out to evacuate these, leaving only a few posts with signal pistols behind. The others, on the other hand, had to hold themselves in readiness in the bunkers that we had dug into the trenches.

A weak wind blew in from the enemy's side, and we anticipated what would come next. The French wafted gas towards us. We knew all about this tactic, since the Germans also used it sometimes. Of course, this was only with the most auspicious weather conditions. A telephone post with a gas mask on one's face doesn't lend itself to operating the apparatus very well, but this circumstance couldn't last forever, and so we were content to insure that the lines were whole until further notice. But an hour later we heard nothing on the telephone. It was about this time that Studt attempted to find the position on the highway. We were forced to go out again and try to find out the cause. A short distance from the road we found the broken line in a bundle

22. French Tank Attack

with other lines, for after our work others had used our relay post to connect other formations. We once more laid the line and when we came to Studt, who was in charge of the telephone, we discovered that we had become connected to the artillery. Studt immediately took it upon himself to go out and correct the mistake.

Soon there came a signal that the line was clear and that Studt was to continue on to the company. At the same time I received the message that our field kitchen was expected to pass by the relay post on its way to the front. The gas attack from the enemy had ceased, but the artillery came to life with heavy fire over the entire territory behind the lines, including the highway where we had our relay post, which was bombarded with shells. Clearly this was the enemy's second stage in preparation for a new attack. I bent my thoughts towards our field kitchen. It had been over a day since our boys had any warm food. And how was I, alone in the telephone cache beneath the old tree to be able to see the approaching kitchen wagon? For the most part, the shelling was intense on the road and I was rather exposed. In such situations, the question of food was as important as protection of my duty. From a telephone conversation between the companies, I heard that an attack was feared from the other side at any time. Dawn began to break now, and the various wagons could be distinguished as they passed on the highway.

Numerous columns with ammunition galloped past, but as far as I could see the highway was sheathed in smoke and mist. One of the boys from the Fourth Company came, and I heard that a French turncoat had revealed the coming French attack. An hour later, one of our comrades arrived and relieved me. Now, I thought, I could seek out our field kitchen on my own. It was certainly mad to go out alone, but one had to try. I didn't dare go more than about five hundred meters, but I saw that it was useless. The French artillery now began an even more ferocious barrage on the foremost trenches. I ran double time back to the bunker in order to be close to my comrades, for the position of being alone was too much to take.

Our field kitchen did not come, but rather we were given permission to break into our reserve rations and partake of a portion thereof. The enemy fire then began to diminish, and our troops were ordered into a state of highest readiness. It was now seven o'clock, and a black cloud had appeared a ways off from the front line trenches. It was the expected attack, but this time with flame-throwers or incendiary weapons. This time there were no tanks. The attackers overran the first and second trenches, and since they were not met with fire from our side, they found the situation incomprehensible. But we knew the score.

As ordered, our machine gun divisions were on guard, and they rose out of the fox holes with their weapons and peppered the attackers with a horrific fire. A close line of French infantry followed the first storm troops, and it was massacred without mercy. In a conversation afterwards in our bunkers, we heard that even the ambushing warriors thought it was a slaughter. But unfortunately, war knows no human law to use against attackers.

During the on-going French attack, a French airman arrived, who apparently was to observe the battle. In his enthusiasm he flew too low and right into the path of the enemy artillery. We only saw the plane shudder and fall down in pieces. We spared no effort to force the enemy to cease their attack, as we hoped.

The unimaginable losses that the enemy endured during the two days must surely have depressed the most optimistic general staff. But the Frenchmen knew what they were fighting for. Even on the same day after all of the losses, new troops gathered on the French side and occupied both of our first-line trenches. It was the Hessian Infantry Regiment who innumerable times demonstrated their bravery. These fighters entered into the fray in order to drive out the enemy from the positions. But the French had become firm of mind to stay put against all circumstances. Our company too received orders to go on the attack with hand grenades. There were hard battles that soon came at close quarters. The artillery could not be called in, for our own would otherwise have become casualties. The enemy fought stubbornly, strengthened at every turn with new troops. But the Hessians were no less stubborn. There were heavy losses on both sides. We were now called by telephone to reinforce the medics from other regiments. When finally, towards evening, we noticed that the offensive strength of the enemy was waning, the French artillery began to fire shells with shrapnel that made further man-on-man combat impossible. The enemy withdrew to no man's land, and we once more occupied our blown-apart trenches.

We counted the soldiers in our company and found that we were forty men less. But fortunately, only a few of them had died. During

22. French Tank Attack

this battle one of our comrades made the observation that another comrade had been wounded shortly before the end of the fight and apparently couldn't fend for himself. He was certain that he didn't know who this comrade was, but he knew approximately the place where the wounded might be lying. It was already dark and he went out alone to seek the comrade. Because it was a dangerous endeavor, he forbade his compatriots to follow. But he went out alone again. A long time passed and one feared the worse for the brave man. For the moment is was quite quiet in no man's land, and at that instant a couple of men hopped out of a trench in order to help with the search. But not far in front of the trenches the machine guns of the enemy began to send some salvos over us. Then, a bit to the right of us some people fell down over the lip of the trench, dragging after them another unconscious body.

It was the man who had risked going out alone, and he actually found what he was looking for; it was a young lieutenant in the infantry. Luckily he wasn't so badly wounded, but he had been shot in both knees and it was impossible for him to move himself. The loss of blood, however, had been serious. For this bravery our diligent comrade received a high commendation and promotion to corporal.

New reinforcements arrived at our part of the front. We ourselves were hardly able to mount a defense and were immediately called to a more quiet part of the front. It was a few kilometers to the north and closer to the Meuse where our next field of work lay.

But before we departed we had to break our lines. The enemy became restless and shot continually at the trucks where we had our relay post. Another of the telephone operators and comrade Studt went out, but after half an hour the other returned and asked for help with Studt, who was wounded. We went out and retrieved him. A piece of shrapnel from a grenade had hit him in the belly and despite immediate help he died the same night among us. It was September 28, 1918.

It was now the fourth and last year of the war—I can tell this now after so many years, but at the time we had ceased to speak of the end of the war. A general malaise had been inculcated among every soldier. We were nothing more than robots that obeyed orders; we were not able to reflect any more. Eat and drink and sleep, that was what interested us the most.

But, now after so many years, I am still able to remember. Among all of the memories of that hard and bloody life at the front there is much that appears so realistically that an honorable soldier can never forget. In the next section I will recall how a portion of the officers who lived behind the front lived during the war.

Within the German army every officer had the right to choose one man from among the troops and to have him as an adjutant. If it was the commander of a company or some other higher officer, he had two or three men to serve him. As far as this person was concerned, it was a great advantage to escape all of the other duties apart from those asked of him. Of course, the adjutants of the command serving at the front were forced to appear beside their commander the entire time that they were in the trenches.

But it is not the life of the officers on the front that I want to describe. Here, this concerns the so-called generals or higher ranks. These usually had their positions further back from the front. This offered them a life with many pleasures, especially in the calmer sectors. The officers never had to eat anything like that which was doled out to us from the field kitchens. They had their own kitchens, and it was normal that one obtained for themselves a butcher as a cook. The military post or special procurement of extra rations and drink were sent far behind the front.

On calmer fronts, an officer's mess was created where one could have the pleasant company of officers from other divisions. We often had the occasion to hear of these feasts while on guard duty. And when the circumstances were right, there were parties with other divisions. Musicians from the company who had their instruments with them were drafted for these occasions. Now, one didn't want to envy these gentlemen their pleasure, were it not for the fact that many times the food of the troops was limited or bad. We ourselves were content with what we had to live on, but only if it was enough. But sometimes it could be too much, and we noticed that the company cook attempted to hide from our view the extra provisions that we could have purchased from the various marketplaces. This was usually a matter of wine and the better smoked meats.

But all in all, I didn't notice the comfortable situation of the officers very much. Sooner or later they were in the same boat as we were and thus would have to stand in line at our field kitchen. But the further one went behind the front the more unbelievable the life was among the officers.

22. French Tank Attack

About three miles behind the front lines there were also French civilians, and for the officers who had their billets there, there was a possibility of living a life no garrison in Germany could offer: cinemas, theaters, and sporting arenas, and, moreover, in the cities were to be found hotels and bordellos that were only visited by the officers. These were mainly the gentlemen who served in the various squadrons and general staff.

These staff officers residing far behind the battle zone had the possibility of procuring food that was meant for those on the front. There were sometimes packages from home that never made it to the troops. We soldiers on the front lines had the right to home leave one time each year. At the railway stations there were always trains ready for those of us on leave. But a third of the train was first and second class, reserved only for the officers.

We arrived at the train and were able to climb aboard already full coaches. Happy to be going home, we never made any comments about the crowding in the train cars. We had with us our baggage, in which we carried something good that would make our relatives at home happy; perhaps some food we purchased with our pay in the marketplace, since such food that was no longer to be found in Germany. But aboard the train were often one or another soldier, who didn't have such worn uniforms as ours. His military accouterments were quite elegant and proper. These were the so-called adjutants, who carried large packages with them. They also looked after even larger packets that were addressed to the families of their officers. And before these adjutants stepped aboard, they often first oversaw the placement of even larger pieces of freight into the baggage car, many of which were often designated as "official."

The adjutants of the officers were allowed home on leave several times each year. If the officer himself had the occasion to travel, he was followed to the train by his adjutant, who helped him manage all of the packages that his commander had with him. One can note that the transport of freight was largest especially during the retreat from France. It was proven that much came into private ownership along the road of retreat back to Germany. At the Anhalt Station in Berlin, where the trains carrying those on leave arrived, one could see many sellers who offered things for sale to the soldiers. There was always something that could be of use.

On the other hand, if one arrived home himself, happy to visit his relatives, he was often met with a lack of some of the most basic necessities people need. There was lots of money, but one couldn't purchase something that was in short supply.

One should not be concerned that there were comrades who were guilty of theft during their leave. It cannot be an injustice to take from the rich in Germany, when they had done it to the poor, displaced population of France.

Chapter 23

The Americans Arrive

In September–October of 1918 the Germans had constructed a cannon that could shell Paris, a distance of twelve miles. The weapons of war were being developed more and more. New dangerous gasses were invented. But we were tired. We had become old during the four years on the front; years that had been taken off of our lives. Actually, we sometimes had the thought, if the war should end or drag out even longer and we continued to live, what would become of us?

The majority of us had a profession that we had to leave when the war called us to arms. This happened just as we needed all of the practice and skill to become contributors to society. Among us were even more pitiable comrades, who the war had wrenched from school benches and who still had years left to complete a diploma.

It was certainly a misleading thought that we could begin to go home, but the continuation of the will to survive, this was our utmost thought. But we had no clue that the end of the war was quite close.

The Germans were still casting people into the huge war machine. But these young soldiers were mere children in our eyes. We were afraid that we would need to take care of them when the situation demanded a man. The education of the pioneers in Germany during the last year of the war was already completed after four weeks. The young ones were recruited in the belief that there would be more German offensives at the front. Upon their arrival at our place, we were dismayed that they asked really childish questions of us that reflected the war propaganda in Germany. The food began to become scarce or less edible. The uniforms did not display any longer the quality that we were used to, and they began to dole out French and English wares that the commanders of the army had confiscated from the enemy territory. Leave was only granted in the most severe emergencies and with indisputable written proof. Half of the wounded comrades were sent back from hospitals to the front.

All of this showed us certainly that there was a great emergency in embattled Germany. But the war must go on, and the appearance of progress must be reported in the German press. Our division lay in reserve at the Siegfried Front in a very hilly terrain. One afternoon in clear weather an entire squadron flew over the front towards us. The planes were in close formation above us at about 500 meters height. For us, it was strange that German planes dared to fly in broad daylight above the front and still not be shot down. About a kilometer in back of us the horses of the division began to graze. Of course, we firmly believed that these were German planes that we saw, for the machines were so much like the German Rumplers, and they flew above the large mass of troops. Moreover, they were not greeted by artillery. But we were somewhat confused when we saw and heard what happened. When the squadron closed in on the place where the horses were grazing, there was whistling in the air and a mass of small fragmentation bombs rained down among the horses. Instantly the majority of the animals lay down sprawled on their haunches. Only now did our aerial defenses spring into action, but the fliers were already long gone and casting their bombs on a new target. Everything that we observed was beyond our comprehension. Why did the enemy try and kill our animals, but completely ignore the large assembly of troops? Yes, this was the beginning of the tactic that our new adversary used. Following an inventory of our horses, the entire division found they had only a third of them left. If at the start we didn't understand this strange occurrence, we would soon find out how difficult a blow it was for the German army. Day and night the Americans harassed the German side in a similar manner. The transportation in trucks of our food supply or the freight cars on the railway, or a bridge or a supply depot were the preferred targets of the enemy.

This made things visible to the greatest degree of how it affected the sustaining of the troops at the front. It was strange to us that only a few human lives were lost by the offensive of the American airmen. If they sighted a transportation column on the road, the enemy aircraft dropped a huge bomb a distance in front of the wagons and blocked all transport.

23. The Americans Arrive

But the enemy also worked in another, so to say bloodless manner. One day, we were on our way in wagons to the front and were in the process of entering the running trenches that led to the defensive line, when we observed a group of soldiers in a wood. They could have been about two hundred in number. But each and every one of them had a bandage in front of their eyes. Our astonishment was great, and we looked about for a reason for this occurrence. The answer was that these soldiers had managed to enter a gas zone, and they suddenly lost their ability to see. According to the doctor's diagnosis, they would get over it but they needed hospital care. The strange thing about it was that these patients simply couldn't see during the daytime, while at night they were able to take off their bandages. This effect lasted three or four weeks. But one can imagine what sort of casualties at the front occurred through this clever battle treatment.

The Germans were forced to retreat under these various circumstances. Reserve positions were fortified, and we were not inclined to surrender, but the Americans discovered our carefully hidden depots and destroyed them with their airplanes. Then there was a slow and certain retreat to new defensive positions.

Our division now served as an auxiliary troop within the army corps and moved from Noyon-Soisson along the Siegfried Front as the Americans expanded their own front lines. We were able to bypass one or another division. During this time we came into contact with the various German peoples and their highly different dialects.

One time we had the occasion to receive a group of young American soldiers who had been taken prisoner in an unsuccessful charge against our front lines. As usual, we tried to engage in a trade exchange with smoked meats for food or other goods that the enemy had in abundance. As we attempted to speak English with them, they answered in German: "Speak German with us, for we know the language." It emerged that these young men came from German families in America and they had enlisted in the service after they had become Americans.

Eventually our division, which during the time had diminished significantly, had no other task than to withdraw and be reinforced again. For all of us this meant a much-welcomed period of rest.

We were to pass eight wonderful days of rest far behind the front in a small French village among the civilian population. This was a completely new environment for us, who had for the most time remained in the Champagne or Argonne region. Already, there nature was abundant in this very mountainous region. The village where we stayed was small with narrow streets and squeezed in among the heights. There were natural springs everywhere on the streets and at each watering place the population had placed stone basins where they fetched their water and did their laundry. It was a wonderful, clear water that ran day and night. It fit the nice stone houses and the clean cobblestone streets. It was a real pleasure for us each morning to be able to bathe in the ice-cold, clear water. The population itself where we were quartered showed an open sympathy for us from the first moment. Despite the poverty that these people live in—the majority of the villagers worked in the stone quarry—they immediately invited us to supper after our arrival and asked if we wouldn't take all our meals together with the families. We shared our food equally with them; the women helped us store our equipment and in the evenings we spent in lively conversation, as much as we were able. There was a thorough human demeanor on their side that did us good. They did not in the least regard us, as was known everywhere else, that we were the enemies of their country. Every now and again one heard the sorrowful expression: "*Oui, c'est la guerre.*"

Now, after eight days, it continued once more as usual. In the evening we listened to the normal orders of the day, and the next morning at six o'clock we stood ready to march on the street. The march went south at a rapid pace. Around midday we neared a railway station and embarked on a train. We had no idea where we were going. The journey still only took about six hours. Then we continued on by road. We arrived once more in the vicinity of the Argonne. We made camp on an open field late and in the dark. An officer from a foreign company arrived then and made us aware that we were right next door to an airfield. But none of us thought anything more about the information. We had already raised our tents and obtained straw in order to bed down, when the company's officer insisted that it was perhaps unhealthy for the company to sleep so near the place where a heavy bomber squadron had its base. The squadron's task was to drop bombs on the larger French cities during the night. But we clearly had no intention of changing the company's camp to another place. And thus we crept into our tents in peace to sleep.

It was around midnight that we were awakened by the horrible

23. The Americans Arrive

sound of a siren. Immediately the anti-aircraft guns sprang to action and we heard the sound of airplanes. It was a French bomber that paid us a visit, and we felt already the concussion of the bombs so close by. Now we had to be quick. Immediately we placed ourselves in safety by spreading out and seeking shelter in the dark wherever we found a ditch or another depression in the earth. The anti-aircraft defenses were quite effective, and soon the enemy plane flew off without causing any real damage.

Then we packed up our tents and went off to a forest nearby, but didn't dare to set up the tents, but rather camped out underneath the trees for the rest of the night. The next day we continued our march and returned once again in the vicinity of the front where we had been before. Orderlies on bicycles had been sent in advance to prepare quarters or camps for the company, but they returned with the negative news that there wasn't any possibility for quarters in the entire district. In this case, we were instructed to camp anywhere we wanted. We dug trenches on a meadow to lie in, with tent canvas and sheets above us. But because we soon would go onwards to the front lines, we had to obtain a place for our baggage wagons. This was worse. The wagons could not stand out in the open so near the front, but we soon solved this problem. On our march we had observed a small hill of birch trees along the way. A few men went over and chopped down the trees, and we drove them to our bivouac. There we placed them in the ground and fastened them with steel wire so that they wouldn't fall over. In this manner we planted a new grove where we could hide our wagons and protect the baggage from any enemy aircraft.

We were once more at the Meuse-Argonne Front. Our troops at the front were quite torn up, and as the only company of pioneers we had much to do. The enemy's unceasing attack had created unrest and nervousness among the infantry. Of course, this regiment was steadfast and was able to defend their battle positions, but at this particular front the French had mingled their attack strength with troops from the colonies, and one was never certain a night attack would not occur.

It was already known to us that the enemy used colored soldiers for defense back in 1914, when the Germans made their surprise advance almost to Paris. At that time fighting was sometimes almost like jungle warfare. The harvest was fully underway in France, and there where the troops advanced across the fields the reaping was already finished and the sheaves erected. During the night the front was guarded with patrols during the offensive. But all too often it seemed that many people went missing. We didn't want to or would not believe that they had been taken prisoner by the enemy, for there was no sound of fighting. But soon soldiers with their throats slit were found everywhere among the standing sheaves of wheat.

It was an insidious war. The colonial soldiers, often black as night in color, hid in the sheaves and acted according to their customs from their wild homelands with only knives as an effective weapon. And here too at the front we found out that numerous skirmishers came during the night. Unseen by the people in the trenches, a group of black men could almost sneak forward and with hand grenades cause a great loss of life. Our nervousness was thus quite well motivated. But due to this tactic we didn't have so much underground work to do, but rather were mostly involved in setting up barbed wire and going on patrol.

The barbed wire always needed to be reinforced and set up anew. But because of the close distance between our trenches and those of the enemy, it was a risky affair to go out into no man's land. Planting the barbed wire meant that one drove iron stakes into the ground and connected them to each other with wire. If we had to replace these iron stakes with new ones at times, then we had to be extremely cautious in how we did it, so that the enemy wasn't able to hear anything. We usually laid a rug over the edges of the iron stakes in order to dampen the sound as we hammered them home. But one place, where I and two comrades were to lay barbed wire, was barely a hundred meters from the enemy positions. We hadn't the slightest idea how we were going to go out there. But after considering the impossible we came to another thought that was also possible.

The enemy's position was somewhat lower than ours and thanks to that coincidence we emerged from the trench. We made a Spanish rider. Thus we unwound the wire in the form of a huge hollow cylinder one meter in diameter and three meters long, fastened it with a few strings and lifted it above the edge of the trench. When it then fell, it rolled by itself down to the old barbed wire. But we were not always fortunate to hit the right place where the wire needed to be fastened, and thus it rolled on further and the enemy was able to use it. Ah well, we had to redo the work, because orders were orders and here we weren't supposed to cheat.

23. The Americans Arrive

As already noted, we also had to work with a neighboring division, and it was there that the attacks by the black troops regularly occurred. Due to the frantic activity, there was significant gunfire at the front and in between the lines in no man's land lay the ruins of houses in a village that had been shot to pieces. There the French patrols had an excellent forward point for their raids and could set up one or another machine gun nest permanently. But as it happened, we could observe with some certainty that only when the French patrols were out did the soldiers provide them with some protection in one direction.

Now one day we received orders to pile out during the night and blow up the ruined walls that hindered the view from our trenches. After a few preparations an entire troop of very able sappers crept away. One after the other sneaked forward allowing for a great distance from one another. The darkness was their only aid, and all movements had to be done silently and cat-like. They were entirely dependent upon themselves, trusting their good luck. They could not count upon help from the positions, for in such cases this would only disturb the enemy. The boys held in front a special device so that nothing would make a click. As weapons, each one had four egg-shaped hand grenades in their pocket. The detonation was to be done by electric wire from the trench, but only after the boys had fulfilled their work and returned to the position. The orders required that the main explosives were placed at a minimum of five points. It was the luck of this mission that the group began to depart just when it was dark enough, otherwise the night time would not have been enough. It was calculated that one or at most two hours would be sufficient. There was complete calm on the side of the enemy, and yes, thinking about it afterwards, a suspicious calm. It was lucky beyond all expectations that the group arrived without being noticed. Then, one only needed to find the proper place in the dark where one could tie the explosives. Now, we had a type of dynamite of high explosive power that didn't need to be packed in.

The time passed, and we in the trench stood and waited tensely. In spite of everything, we were also prepared to jump to their rescue if a tumult were to ensue. Soon it had taken too long a time for us to wait, but the orders had to be carried out. Just then, when the calculated time for action had passed, fire burst forth from the enemy like a little hell. Every place they could have put machine guns seemed to be in motion on the opposite side.

There we stood in our trenches and had nothing else to do but to protect ourselves from the hailstorm of small projectiles that passed over our heads. We were not afraid that this was the beginning of a continuous attack by the enemy, but how did our boys fare?

The intensive fire lasted about an hour, when it suddenly ceased. Now all that had to be done was to keep watch on the entire area to see what would happen. A few moments after this insane fire stopped we heard movement right in front of us and a panting voice: "Light it off, light it off—the French are coming!" It was our guys, and everyone arrived back in good shape, but out of breath. The next instant we heard and saw a huge detonation among the ruins. We had successfully connected the electricity to the explosive wires. The mission had succeeded. But the boys had observed and by now we too understood that the enemy was coming. And these were not just a few, but rather at least an entire company. Luckily, we were all at our posts and could meet the charge with our warmest response. Here too, there were once more a large number of blacks who ran towards us and fell before our weapons. It really was a terrible sight for us to see these black troops come running and falling. We had the impression that they stormed forward like animals without a thought towards taking cover somewhere. Even though we pitied the charging opponents that fell before our weapons, it was almost a relief for us to be rid of those blacks one way or another.

Further off to the left of us an infantry regiment was relieved by a Bavarian regiment. During my field service I had the occasion to make some observations about the temperament of the people. In their homeland—Bavaria—it was naturally quite pretty, but for the most part it was rough country dominated by mountains, and this had set its stamp upon these people. The men that I met in the field were for the most part reticent, but very energetic. There was no problem with their discipline, but their stubbornness was quite recognizable on various occasions.

It was on the English front where a permanent no man's land separated both trenches—the German and the English—by only ten meters wide. The English, like the Germans, made no attacks there. The warfare was conducted mostly with the casting of hand grenades, and now and then small mines. But because this was too limited for the enemy, or for whatever other reason there might have been, the English began

23. The Americans Arrive

to bombard the German side with everything they had that didn't relate to the serious war situation. They shot a type of homemade projectile filled with unpleasant stinking garbage or old tins with sharp edges onto the German soldiers. This was tolerated a long time until the Bavarians relieved the men in the trenches.

This mischief went on for a time until the Bavarians, who no longer wanted to participate in the joke any further, one fine day took off their tunics, tucked up their shirttails, and each man armed himself with a cudgel. Then and there they sprang out of the trenches, ran on over to the enemy, gave them a good thrashing in their trenches, and took a few prisoners.

In another place on the front, the Bavarian infantry also had a hard fought battle with the English, but at last the enemy surrendered and a number of prisoners were taken. When the prisoners had arrived at the German side, an English corporal reached out his fist towards a Bavarian soldier as if to thank him for a good match. But the Bavarian, who didn't think much of this sport and knew how many of his comrades were relieved of their lives, slapped the English corporal upside the head.

One time, at a Bavarian position on the front, the King of Bavaria's birthday was to be celebrated. The day of this honor the personnel were to have roast lamb to eat along with those dumplings that the Bavarians all love. Afterwards, the company was to be gathered for a toast. The men got their food, but they didn't receive along with it that which they desired most—beer. It was inconceivable to offer this folk anything better than beer. The result was that the chef had to store almost all of the food, and the rest came to the gathering with a sour disposition. The commandant, who otherwise was quite particular about his men, hastily obtained the much-desired beer for the evening, and calm was re-established in the company.

But with respect to the battle on the front against the black colonial troops, I must report something here on account of the Bavarian soldiers, which casts a black shadow upon them. This occurred on the Champagne Front outside the city of Reims. They succeeded in making an attack and had advanced into the city. But the German commanders at the front had not been warned that the French had many colored regiments. Here too, the Bavarian troops fought bravely. I do not know whether the army commanders anticipated difficulties in taking the city, but the orders were to bypass the town. After a hard battle they succeeded in driving back the enemy, but afterwards the city itself had to be cleansed of the remaining French. This led to one of the most difficult actions during the World War. If the troops as a whole could report good success, the Bavarians lost a huge strength of their own in the cleansing. And the most tragic part of it was that the soldiers were attacked by the black troops and many were murdered from behind. The bitterness was limitless concerning this, and when at last the enemy was overcome, the Bavarians took no blacks prisoner, but rather shot every single Negro.

Here at the Meuse-Argonne Front, the Bavarians were quite significant in terms of the defense. When it seemed hopeless to resist the enemy pressure, these soldiers fought with indescribable tenacity. Soon, we too had to retreat from the front here, and we pioneers were ordered to dig new defensive positions further back. We were taken to a half ruined work camp that had long since been abandoned by a weapons battalion. From there we had to go on our daily marches to work. The rations were once more rotten, and we knew ourselves that we couldn't continue this heavy work that took the starch out of us.

One morning we went off to our workplace again. The new position that we had excavated lay so far away from the first lines of battle that there was no risk for us. After a mug of coffee and bit of bread we staggered off, one platoon strong. As commanders we had, apart from our corporals, Lieutenant Küsters. This officer was the most zealous person possible, who demanded the utmost possible from his personnel, both in terms of work and battle. For him, nothing was impossible. But he never spared himself, whatever task lay before him. On a day patrol with a few men to seek out a new path towards the front, a pause was called in order to eat a bite of food. We took out our bread and spread on it some thin marmalade. He too took out his packet of sandwiches that his adjutant had made for him. On his sandwiches there was, apart from good butter, various tasty morsels. When he saw how meager our bread with marmalade was in comparison with his, he became angry. He divided his sandwich in pieces, and we gave him some of ours. Upon the return to the camp he sought out his adjutant and this man had to serve in the company for a week as punishment. Likewise, he quite seldom partook of the succulent offerings that the cook provided his officers.

23. The Americans Arrive

Now, as I said before, we were at our workplace behind the front. When we laid down our rifles, we grabbed the shovels and hacked about and worked for awhile. The earth was hard and quite often we had to pause to rest. During just one of the pauses the lieutenant arrived and wondered why we were standing there, resting on our tools. The answer, naturally, was that we could not go so long at one stretch. We were, quite simply, too hungry. But then he advised us: "Tighten your belts a little more, and then you will be able to do it." Sure, we could think of nothing else than "he is an idiot." But in time even our commander recognized that we couldn't be forced to do such intensive work with such poor sustenance, and thus we received as much as wished.

On another occasion we were to lie in reserve in a trench in back of the first front line. This was also under the command of Küsters. Right in front of us was a hill so that we had no line of sight towards the front lines. There the battle raged intensely, but we were shelled heavily by rifle bullets that dropped down on us. The post was dug in such short proximity in order to give the alarm when the danger of a breakthrough was imminent. Of course, the people stationed there sought shelter behind the breastworks against the shells. Lieutenant Küsters observed this and ordered that the soldiers should stand upright with half their bodies unprotected against the enemy, even though a view forward was impossible because of the hill. The lieutenant's order was issued with the threat that he would immediately shoot anyone who hid behind the shield. Those posted there nonetheless knew when we would become involved, for the eventual retreating forces there would have become visible in enough time. But at the orders of the officer, all of a sudden the respect completely collapsed, and an old solider went up to the lieutenant saying: "Shoot, shoot as many as you can, for the faster you do, the faster the war is over for us." The lieutenant certainly understood the idiocy of the order and repealed it.

Finally, among many in all the forces at the front there was a natural rebellion against everything that one considered to be unjustified. It was quite simple the opinion of the people not to regard this as some insubordination or even a mutiny. One time our company received a new requisition of uniforms. The tunics were poorly constructed, as was everything else. This was also the same for our stockings. The boots that we got, however, were of good quality and we were quite happy to have them. That same evening a platoon had to go out to the battle lines and work as usual. Towards morning the platoon returned back and had a comrade with them who had been killed during the night by an enemy bullet. This comrade was a vice-corporal in the company, quite well regarded and liked by us for his loyalty and sense of justice.

The company commander, doctor, and paymaster arrived to see the corpse. The latter commented that it was certainly too bad to allow the nice boots that the dead man had on him to be put with him into his grave. The company commander then gave two men orders to take off the footwear of the fallen man. They attempted to follow the orders, but however much they pulled (and perhaps they thought this was barbaric), all attempts were in vain and the boots stayed on. Then it was decided that the company cobbler would slice up the boot laces, and thereafter one could remove them. We knew all about the commander and his sometimes completely absurd orders. The cobbler himself didn't think that it was any way to treat the dead, not to bury him with all of his clothes. The cobbler began to carry out the orders, but let his comrades know about them. This was too much for us. We assembled all together at the depot where the dead man lay and prevented the cobbler from fulfilling his duty. And, in turn, all he could do was to report this to the commander.

The company commander arrived and with all of his power tried to insist on the orders. The closeness of all of us made him a bit stubborn, but in our faces it was not difficult for him to read our take on the matter. Finally, one of us stepped forward and clearly expressed to the officer that the dead man should retain his damned boots that he had been happy to have while he was alive. The commander could do nothing else but turn his back to us in embarrassment and trot off in silence.

Chapter 24

The Last Events and Close

My last diary entries date from the period September 27th to October 18, 1918, during the battle on the Meuse. But there was little to report on the choreographic organization and precise data. We still had unpleasant skirmishes at the front. At the end our hopeless position was also known to the French. But the French troops themselves were not able to mount an offensive, and their desire at the very least to drive us out completely from the country was not able to be undertaken, thanks to the decimation of the French army.

Here fate had to intervene and make an end to the war. And it came without us wanting to believe in such a long-desired conclusion, for our minds were dulled by the thought that it would ever come. At the very end we had the last losses to note: three dead and five wounded. Among the latter was Lieutenant Küsters. He received a nasty bullet wound in the calf, and we carried him to the ambulance. His last words to us were: "What will happen to the company when I am no longer with them?" We who heard them could only smile in answer. His zealousness and huge belief in himself could not be suppressed, even though he lay on a stretcher. Long afterwards we learned moreover that he had his leg amputated at the hospital. His faith as a soldier must finally have been little more than a joke by then.

The lack of people in the army must have been unprecedented. The wounded who did not display any very serious wounds were no longer allowed to leave the company for hospital care. Medically trained youngsters were moved in to assist the personnel in the company. The communal room, an old barrack, was assigned. Only the sick received better rations, which for the most part consisted of a larger bread ration and margarine, as well as oatmeal. A prohibition against leave was instituted.

At home in Germany there was a huge dearth of food, and the last ones to return from leave who came back spoke of troops in the garrisons who refused to serve unless their relatives back home received the opportunity to buy more food.

One of the largest and most read satirical papers, *Simplicissimus*, had on its title page one day a hill of bones and skulls with the moneylenders sitting on top. Underneath the picture was the text: "Enough is enough!" And the weeping figure trying to buy it gave people much to think about.

The last days of October we once more were formed into a column and marched to the nearest railway station. We were stuffed into boxcars and other railway wagons, and then taken off on a ten-hour journey back across the border to Germany. At first we understood that the

Railway station with soldiers awaiting a troop train back to German territory, October 1918 (photograph by Artur H. Boer; van Boer family archives).

24. The Last Events and Close

entire division was to be filled out with fresh troops from the garrisons in Germany. Then we were to be taken next to the area around Strasbourg to be put in where hard fighting against the American troops was in progress. Due to our old experience we were not optimistic, even though the transportation went across the German border. A rumor had no influence upon us anymore. But nonetheless, to return to German territory once more filled us with a feeling of happy caution.

The train with us stopped in the city of Neunkirchen, and we actually thought we were going to be allowed to stay for a certain period of time. We didn't care where we would continue on to in the slightest. As a group, we were quartered among the German civilian population, and these people received us in the most heartfelt manner. We really lived it up again, for we could now once more behave like normal people and had access to baths and could wash daily. It didn't disturb us in the least that the quarters could not offer each and every one a nice place to sleep. The kindness of the people replaced anything some comfort could offer.

After we had rested completely for a few days we drilled on a meadow outside the city for a few hours each day. After about a week our company was increased with some thirty or so young boys from our garrison in Stettin. We thought of ourselves as uncles compared to these young pioneers, who were barely eighteen and twenty years old. Now there was daily exercise in the mornings and instruction for the entire company in the afternoons. But even here in this nice, quiet city we were not spared an accident. A couple of the young pioneers were blown up by hand grenades. To get the young newcomers used to explosive ammunition, we had the occasional practice casting hand grenades. Without anyone's knowledge, one evening two of the boys went down to the river that flowed through the city to catch fish using hand grenades. Incompletely educated in these weapons, they were found dead before they even approached the front. Unfortunately, everything was done in secret, and there were no witnesses who could say how it had happened.

The relatives of the boys immediately received the news and in their, the company's, and the townspeople's presence, we had a funeral in the city cemetery that one will never forget.

After visiting for fourteen days we said good-bye to the city's nice people and boarded a military transport train. The journey went south, and as was now certain to us, towards the Strasbourg Front. This portion of the front was one of the only ones that lay so close to Germany. But we still did not have an idea of what the coming days would surprise us with. It was November 18, 1918.

After a day's journey our train suddenly slowed down at four o'clock in the afternoon. We saw that it was coming closer to another train on the next track, which was giving the signal to our engineer to stop. When both trains met, several soldiers got off of the train meeting us. These German soldiers had no rank markings, but rather only had red armbands on their left arms. Likewise, their caps were encircled with a red cockade. An older man, who from the look of him and his bearing was an officer, asked after our officers. Of course, everyone in our train was wondering what the reason was for our stopping, and as many as there were got off. We gathered in the proximity of our coaches in which our officers were traveling and learned with anxiety that a revolution was going on in Germany. We learned that the German Kaiser had abdicated and that the people were being governed by people who had been elected. The person who spoke was an officer who belonged to the revolutionary army. Our company was questioned on whether we were willing to leave the front entirely and travel home.

This was the greatest moment in a soldier's life. With jubilation we took advantage of this instance to be able to be finished with that insane life that we had been forced to lead. The revolutionary officer explained the entire situation in curt phrases, asked that our officers hand over their weapons, and determined that our company elect new leadership, a council of soldiers according to the rules of the revolution.

Our officers made no complaints, and the company chose on the spot four men who would take care of the continuing transportation to our home garrison. How the morale was among our officers in reality is not rightfully known. Upon first impression they appeared to be almost calm, but they had little impact upon the situation. They were, so to speak, uncoupled from all responsibility and put under guard by their own men.

For ourselves it was a bit incomprehensible that from now on we had to rely on one of our corporals, who was the lead spokesman for us. The troop train went on. On the way to our garrison we arrived at a little station for our first refreshments. There we received warm food

24. The Last Events and Close

from a field kitchen that was run by the German Women's Defense Forces, who also wore red armbands. Everything when we arrived was indicative of the revolution. But here during our mess we experienced a surprise. As we were standing in line with our mess kits, our company commander was last, followed by the remaining gentlemen, each with their plate, to obtain the warm soup just like us. And following the officers came their adjutants.

This sight gave us a feeling of peace, as well as a sort of satisfaction, and we saw that our officers followed the new order without opposition. From this point on we now felt even more compassion for them. Now we knew that their previous comradeship with us was truly the real thing.

Certainly, the officers underwent additional interrogation at each stop where the soldier's council at the place wanted to determine the loyalty of the company. But each time we could anticipate that the officers were with us.

At one of the many train stations where several of those empowered by the revolution spoke to the officers, all of a sudden our doctor stepped forward with a small pistol in his hand, saying: "It is true that I forgot to surrender this here. Perhaps the new army has a use for it?" Everyone who saw and heard this broke out laughing, and one of the men assured the doctor that he could gladly keep his toy. He would not be able to prevent the revolution with it.

Our last train journey in the military lasted for several days. In Germany, it had already been known long since how the war was going to end. But the moment the Kaiser left and fled the country, in many respects the situation was completely chaotic. This was also the case with the entire rail system. Our train had to stop from time to time because other trains had to be rerouted (sometimes among them many originally on their way to the front). But everywhere we met people. With every stop people appeared who wanted to hear from us how it looked over there in France at the end of the fighting. But unfortunately we couldn't tell them anything, for we were safely away before that point in time.

It was moving for us to recognize the happiness with which we were received. Every person was filled with an enthusiasm, and even a few war veterans from 1870–1871 wanted to speak with us. Everywhere the red flag of revolution was raised. Everywhere we were met with gifts in the form of fruit and foodstuff. We were all moved. But not all people were able to participate in the general thoughts of joy. I also saw tearful faces. These were mothers and girls who mourned a son, a brother, and husband, who perhaps not so long ago had died in a foreign land.

Finally, after many days our troop train passed through Berlin, the German capital. The train was destined for our garrison city of Stettin, which was still several hours away, but my home was Berlin, where I had my mother and sister. Thus it was understandable that I longed to go home to them as quickly as possible.

I requested to stop my journey and made a detour to my home outside of the capital. What I most wanted to avoid was something that at the time filled me with sorrow and trepidation. There, on Berlin's streets was occurring an on-going struggle among the people whether it was the German republic's fate "to be or not to be."

Index

Numbers in ***bold italics*** indicate illustrations.

adjutants 166–167
aircraft 31–34, 79, 122, 144, 151–153, 173; Fokker triplane 33; German Rumpler 35, 170
Aisne River 11, 100, 143
All Quiet on the Western Front 8
Allenstein 9, 56
Allied Blockade of Germany 35–36, 45
ambulance wagons 68
Americans 15, 17–18, 44, 170–171
ammunition depot 120–123
anti-tank guns 158
ants 104
Antwerp (Belgium) 55
Argonne campaign/Front 31, 147; *see also* Argonne region
Argonne region 16, 44, 143, ***145***, 156–157, 172
Armistice (1918) 14
Artur's father 3–4, 92
aviators 144, 151, 154; American 170–171; English 17, 149–153; French 115, 121, 145, 164, 173; German 149–153, 172; Russian 74

balloons 31–32, 96, 144, 148, 150
Bapaume (France) 11, 33, 148
Bavaria, King of 177
Bavarian troops 17, 19, 84, 176–178
Berlin 4, 11, 15, 42, 45, 53, 92, 167, 186; Anhalt station 167
Bismarck, Otto von, Chancellor of Germany 43

Boer, Artur—depicted ***ii***, ***57***, ***133***, ***157***
Bofors *see* Karlskoga
Bois de Caillette (France) 11, 25, 38, 40, 113, 115, 118, 124
Brocken *see* Harz Mountains

Cambrai (France) 11, 148
Canal de Crozat (France) 11, 138, 140
Canal de Picardie *see* Canal de Crozat
Champagne (province) 11, 16, 31–32, 42, 94–95, 97, 108, 131, 172; Champagne Front 19, 120, 177; *Champagne pédiculaire* 95; *Luschampagne* 95
chaplain 109
Charleville (France) 11, 42, 94
Chemin des Dames (France) 11, 13, 34, 38, 110, ***133***, 134, 136, 154
Chevel de Frise see Spanish riders
church bells 155
Colonial troops (Allies) 15, 18–19, 173–174, 178; Africans 19, 20, 178; Indochinese 19; Madagascans 19; Maghrebins 19
Czerwena Gora (Black Road) 9, 62

Danzig (now Poland) 56
Derik (comrade at Wernigerode) 89
dogs 104–105
Doumont (France) 11, 112, 115

East Prussia 56
Eastern Front 9, 21, 29, 33, 36, 39, 41, 44, 56, 71, 83
Eierhandgranate see hand grenades

187

Index

Eighth Company, 66th Regiment (German Army) 116
Elizabeth (nurse at Wernigerode) 89–90

family graves (as bivouacs) 142
Feldhaubitze see howitzer
flack cannon (anti-aircraft gun) 31, 74
Flanders 147
food 155, 169, 172, 178–179, 184–186; *see also* rations
rations 161, 163, 178, 182; *see also* food
Franz Josef, Austro-Hungarian Emperor 53
French Front *see* Western Front
Friedrich Wilhelm, Crown Prince of the German Empire 27–28, 107
Fürster, Lieutenant 141

Gabelsberger system 5, 42, 90
German Confederation 43
German press 170; *see also Simplicissimus*
German Reich 48
German soldiers—depicted *110*, *133*, *145*, *157*
German Women's Defense Forces 185
Geyer, Lieutenant 116–117
Granatschrapnell 29

hand grenades 29, 59, 65, 68, 78, 80, 98, 134, 158, 175
Harz Mountains 10, 42, 88–90; Brocken (mountain) 42, 90
Hessian Infantry Regiment 79, 164
Hindenburg, Field Marshal Paul von 9, 56
Hindenburg Line *see* Siegfried Line
Höhle, Karl 118–119
Höllenschlucht (Hell's Glen) 125, *126*
howitzer 29, 62, 71, 134, 159, 169

Jarotschin (Jarocin) 3
Jednorzec (Russia) 66

Karlskoga (Sweden) 1–4; Bofors 2, 4; *Nerikes Allehanda* 2
Kasemattenschlacht 112
Kiel (Germany) 45
Kluge, Klara 4
Kreuzburg fortress *see* Rózan
Kumla 1–2
Küsters, Lieutenant 25–27, 116, 178–179
Küster's camp 41, 88, 90

Lange Max (*Big Bertha*) *see* howitzer
Laon (France) 11
Latin 130
Lenin, Vladimir 44
Lens (France) 11
Lice *see* Lousoleum
Liège (Belgium) 55
Lousoleum 39, 103

Maas River *see* Meuse River
machine guns 28, 67, 72, 78, 80–81, 114, 134, 144, 152, 158, 164–165
Magdeburg 138
Marne Offensive 109
Materialschlacht 44
Meuse River 43, 143, 156–157, 181
Meuse-Argonne Front 18, 23, 25, 156–157, 173, 178; Battle on the Meuse 181
mines 79, 120, 134, 145
Mont Didier (France) 17
Mont Didier Front 17
music making 3–4, 24, 89, *157*, 166

Namur (Belgium) 55
Narev River 11, 79, 81
narrow gauge railway *126*
Nerikes Allehanda see Karlskoga
Neunkirchen (Rhineland, Germany) 15, 45, 183
Nicholas II, Czar 16, 61
Noyon-Mt. Didier Front 148
Noyon-Soisson 171; *see also* Noyon-Mt. Didier Front; Soisson

Oder River 10, 92
officers 70, 133, 166–167, 180, 184–185; *Offizierhaß* (hate of officers) 24, 28; *see also* Fürster, Lieutenant; Küsters, Lieutenant
Olsztyn *see* Allenstein
Orest, Elsa Linnea 4
Orzic River 10, 73
Osterode (Germany) 10, 41, 87
Ostrolenka (Russia) 74, 77, 79
owl 98–99

Paris 30, 56, 169, 173
Paul (invalid and musician in Wernigerode) 90
Picht, Werner 44
Pioneer Corps 4, 20, 79, *133*, 183
Plonjava (Poland) 10
Podossje (Poland) 10

Index

poison gas 30, 34–35, 134–135, 147, 162
Polish Jews 85
Posen (formerly Prussia) 4
post-traumatic stress disorder 41
potatoes, stealing of 70
prisoners of war 63–64, 129–130
Prasznic (Przasnysz, Poland) 9–10, 40, 62, 72, 85
Przasnysz *see* Prasznic
Pultuska (Russia) 74, 77, 79

Races guerrières (*non-guerrières*) *see* Colonial troops
railways 23, 55–56, 66, 85–86, 87–88, 94, 154–155, 167, 172, *182*, 182–185
rats 104
Red Baron *see* Richthofen, Baron Manfred von
Red Cross 58, 84, 144
Reger, Max (composer) 90
Reims (France) 11, 19, 99, 108, 177; Reims cathedral 99
Remarque, Erich Maria 8
Richthofen, Baron Manfred von 6, 33–34, 148–150
Royal Academy of Engineering 4
Royal Prussian State Railways 4
Rózan (Poland) 10, 40, 74, 77, 79–82; Kreuzberg fortress 10, 33, 74–75, 77
Russian Front *see* Eastern Front

St. Christ (France) 11, 137, 140, 142
St. Petersburg (Russia) 56
Schlanke Emma see howitzer
Seventh Reserve Division (German Army) 154; Fourth Company 160, 162–163
shell shock *see* post-traumatic stress disorder
Siberian elite troops 68
Siegfried Line/Front 11, 15, 157, 170–171
Simplicissimus (German magazine) 47, 182
Sister Elisabeth (nurse at Wernigerode) 90–91

Sitzkrieg 156
Soissons (France) 152
Somme River 12, 137; Battle of Somme 11; Somme Front 137
Spanish riders (barbed wire) 21, 174
Spring Offensive (1918) 11
Springer, Lina 4
Stegna (Russia) 66
Stettin 9–10, 15, 20, 42, 45, 92, 94, 183, 186
Stielhandgranate see hand grenades
Strasbourg (France) 43, 45; Strasbourg Front 183–184
Studt, Comrade (telephone operator) 141, 161–163, 165
Szla (Poland) 9, 72–73

Tahure (Sommepy-Tahure, France) 11, 43, 96, 99
tanks 30–31, 159–160; British Mark I 30; French Char Saint Charmond 30; French Schneider CA 30
tank traps 20, 160
Tannenberg, Battle of 9, 46
Tergnier (France) 15, 137, 140
30.5 Coastal artillery 74
Thorn (city) 9, 56
Toupes de choc 18
Treaty of Brest-Litovsk 44
Turkey (Turks) 71

Vaux (France) 112, 115
Verdun (France) 11, 28, 107, *126*, 129; Battle of Verdun 11, 107

Warsaw 9
Weimar Republic 44
Wernigerode 10, 41, 89
Western Front 11, 16, 21, 23, 37–38, 42–44, 46, 94, 103, 106–107, 124, 154
Wilhelm, Kaiser 15, 43–44, 46, 61, 184–185
wine (wine cellars) 155

Zeppelin 32

www.ingramcontent.com/pod-product-compliance
Ingram Content Group UK Ltd.
Pitfield, Milton Keynes, MK11 3LW, UK
UKHW042012140426
5217IPUK00015B/1118